JAMMU KASHMIR

NAGAR

CHINA

HIMACHAL PRADESH

SIMLA

PUNJAB

DELHI

UTTAR PRADESH

PUR

LUCKNOW

SIKKIM
GANGTOK

PUNAKHA

BHUTAN

ASSAM

NAGALAND

SHILLONG

MANIPUR

IMPHAL

PATNA

GANGES

PAKISTAN

BIHAR

AGARTALA

BHOPAL

MADHYA PRADESH

WEST BENGAL

RIVER

TRIPURA

N D I A

CALCUTTA

ORISSA

HTRA

BHUBANESWAR

HYDERABAD

ANDHRA PRADESH

SORE

Bay

of

Bengal

BANGALORE

MADRAS

MADRAS

COCHIN

RALA

IVANDRUM

CEYLON

Indian Ocean

The Art of
India's Cookery

The Art of
INDIA'S COOKERY

William I. Kaufman

&

Saraswathi Lakshmanan

GARDEN CITY, NEW YORK

Doubleday & Company, Inc.

Foreword

With the countries of the world drawing closer and closer in terms of travel accessibility and cultural exchange, it is inevitable that there would be a growing desire to develop more than a passing acquaintance with the foods of other peoples too. From a cursory glance at the shelves in grocery stores, even in the smaller towns, it is evident that foods of other lands are becoming more and more an integral part of the American culinary repertoire. An increasing number of restaurants nowadays are featuring Indian curries, which are gaining in popularity, giving further proof of the cosmopolitan American palate.

A study of this book will convince one that an Indian dish is not a mysterious concoction that needs the practiced hand of an international chef or an Indian housewife steeped in the culinary tradition of her country, but one that can be whipped up by almost anyone who has the urge to pamper his taste buds with an exotic culinary experience.

Since curry is thought of in the West as being synonymous with Indian food, it is particularly apt that the major portion of this book is devoted to curries. However, since this is no more true than the idea that chop suey represents the cookery of China, it is gratifying to see that recipes for a varied assortment of the other types of Indian foods have an important place in this book too.

Come to think of it, I am sure an Indian housewife would find in these pages all she needs in the way of recipes to earn her an enviable reputation as a versatile cook of all the regional styles of Indian cuisine.

Speaking for myself, I am delighted to have access to a book which not only contains recipes representative of all parts of my country, but one which interprets the ingredients in a format that is convenient to follow especially in the environment of this country which has been my home for the past decade.

From what I know of the experience of many American friends who have tried their hands at cooking Indian dishes, I am confident that not only they, but countless others, will welcome this book as an invaluable addition to their kitchen library.

SHIREEN SUBRAMANYA

ACKNOWLEDGMENTS

This book is a result of the expression "Hands across the sea." Without the co-operation of Mr. P. L. Tandon, Chairman of the Board, Hindustan Lever Limited, Mr. K. N. Miles, and Mr. B. B. Mundkur, Advertising Manager, Foods Division, Hindustan Lever Limited, for permission to use material from the *Dalda Cookbook*, this book would not have the advantage of test-kitchen accuracy which it possesses. The *Dalda Cookbook* has been created as a service to the housewives of India by the Foods Division, Hindustan Lever Limited, Bombay, India.

Special thanks to Mr. and Mrs. Kamal Wath Wahal, Mrs. Indira Khanna, Mrs. Girdhari Lal Gosain, and Mrs. Tara Patwardan. To Mrs. Avennelle S. Day and Miss Lillie Stuckey of the American Spice Trade Association, a special gratitude for helping with their vast knowledge of the why and how of spices.

The help and information provided by the India Tourist Board was invaluable in making this book authentic and understandable.

Contents

12   *Contents*

Introduction

What is Indian cooking? One might as well ask, "What is the ocean?" The ocean is the sum of all its rivers flowing together to cover three quarters of the earth. So it is with Indian cooking . . . the sum of all influences which flow toward the center—Greeks, Kushans, Huns, Chinese, Far Eastern seamen, the Phoenicians, the Muslims, and Europeans—all have fused their cookery into the national cuisine. Each has lost its own identity under the spell of spice. Indian cookery is a variety of food ideas, combinations of nuts with meat, fruit with vegetables, sugar with chili; different meats in different sauces, cooked by different methods borrowed from every invader—all bearing the special stamp of India—spice.

These spices are as varied as the Indian people themselves and the climates in which they live. India has been spice grower to the world for at least 3500 years. For centuries cargoes of spice traveled west on ships bringing gold, gems, and silks. Today, in India, 2,250,000 acres of land are devoted to spice production. India uses a great deal of its big spice crop, but the total yield is large enough to make spices one of the country's most important exports.

The Indian cuisine gets its characteristic flavor and aroma from cardamom, coriander, cumin, and fennel seeds, turmeric, saffron, black and white pepper, cloves, the ever present chilies (hot peppers) and the great curry powder—background seasoning for hundreds of dishes bearing its name and making up an entire category of foods.

Indian cooks insist that these spices be cooked at the temperature of hot fat, not just heated in liquid as is our custom, and this is one of the broad features of this cuisine although the bill of fare changes so much from Kashmir in the North to Malabar in the South and from Eastern India to the Western Ghats, that it is unlikely that any comparable area in the world has such a great variety of dishes. Not many of them can be called "typical" as a result of this variation but there are certain general practices of cooking in India, the knowledge of which will help us to better understand and appreciate Indian cuisine.

Most Indian dishes are prepared in oil or fat. (Ghee, clarified butter, in the North; mustard oil in the East; coconut and gingili oil in the South; and til oil or sweet oil in the West.) Hydrogenated vegetable oil is also largely used though animal fats such as lard are largely avoided. Spices and herbs are used in different combinations for most dishes according to the region in which they are prepared but they are always present. The common notion that *all* Indian dishes are "hot" because of their use is not correct. Salt and pepper or chilies are added to the food while it is being cooked; not sprinkled over at the time of eating.

Since a large proportion of people in India are vegetarians and do not eat meat, fish, or eggs (many do not even take onions or garlic because of their pungent taste), it is indeed fortunate that such a large variety of vegetables is available and that there exist so many ways of cooking them.

A most important category of Indian food is the group of dishes which use a base of milk product such as yogurt or cheese. Thinly grated vegetables, boiled or raw, mixed in beaten curds and garnished with salt, pepper, and green coriander leaves is a popular dish of this kind and it is interesting to note that yogurt in one form or another is eaten in most Indian homes with at least one meal every day.

There is no special order in which Indian dishes are served. Rice, curries, wheat breads called chapaties, vegetables, curds, pickles are all served at the same time. Of course sweets are saved for the last part of the meal.

Indian cuisine uses a preponderance of cereal foods such as rice, wheat, and maize. In South and East India rice is the mainstay of the meal and chapaties made from wheat, maize, and corn meal are basic food in the North and West. Everywhere, a dish of lentils cooked in water, known as *dal*, is served.

The sweet dishes which usually round off an Indian meal are

halwa or *kheer*. For making *halwa*, which can be prepared from carrots, pumpkins, lentils, wheat, flour, and farina, the ingredients are fried well in butter or oil and then cooked with syrup. This preparation is usually garnished with chopped almonds, raisins, cardamoms, saffron, and pistachios. In some cases, *khoa* is added to make the *halwa* richer. *Kheer* is made by adding rice or vermicelli, or carrots, or farina, to a large quantity of milk and letting it simmer on the fire until it attains a nice, thick, rich consistency. Sugar and nuts are added after it has been taken from the fire.

Indian curries are neither fiery, ulcer-forming creations nor are they the pallid boiled rice and chicken with a dash of curry powder which sometimes masquerades under this title. Rightly prepared, curry is subtle and pleasing and just hot enough to be tasty. The proportion of spices varies with each particular dish. Since every spice used in the curry has a special quality, the aim in determining the proportion of each is to achieve a balanced but individual effect.

The cooking being so varied, maybe it might not be a bad idea to take a little travelogue of foods in the four sections of this vast land.

NORTH INDIA

Let us start with the capital, New Delhi, the center of the North Indian type of cooking which is now becoming increasingly popular throughout India. This type of food is served at government banquets and in most of the restaurants and hotels throughout the land. It has quality and richness which reflect the resplendent glory of the past and is popularly called Mughlai food. Wheat and wheat products are its staples. The airy, light chapaties, sometimes known as *phulkas* would remind us of the Mexican tortilla in appearance. They are eaten with cooked vegetables, meat, or lentils. Variations of the chapaties are *parathas* which are shallow fried and served plain or stuffed with vegetables, and *nan* which is slightly leavened dough, flattened and baked dry. *Nan* is very popular and is eaten frequently with spiced, barbecued chicken.

Some favorite curries enjoyed by the North people are *korma*— a rich, thick brown curry made with poppy seeds and dried coconut having meat which is tenderized by being marinated in yogurt— and *roghan josh*, made with a thinner gravy which is deeper red in color. It is made with leg of lamb, cut into fairly large pieces and flavored with saffron added just before the curry is removed from the fire. Kebab curries of all kinds are very popular in North India and make an ideal type of curry for the American cook to use as a starter in her explorations of this exotic and exciting food. Kebabs are pieces of meat, fish, poultry, seafood etc.; sometimes even meatballs made from these ingredients are minced with vegetables, spices, lentils, and threaded on short skewers. They are good cooked in a variety of ways in many of the different, traditional curry sauces.

In North India rice is served in various forms at all parties and in hotels and restaurants. The two main rice preparations are *pulao* and *biryani*. For *pulao* the rice is fried in hot fat or vegetable oil, and cooked in meat stock or hot water. A *bouquet garni* of cinnamon, cardamom, and bay leaves is always added. A *pulao* which has been well prepared should not be greasy nor too hot tasting but should be subtle and pleasing in flavor. Generally, the name of the particular *pulao* is derived from its main ingredient. *Biryani* is richer. The rice is three fourths boiled; a rich curry is prepared with lamb, chicken, or vegetables, and the rice and curry are put in layers in a pan. Fat and milk are sprinkled over it, and the lid is put on and made airtight. The entire dish is then baked. When ready, it is served in dishes with a garnishing of fried nuts, crisply fried onions, raisins, sliced boiled eggs, and, sometimes, it is topped with extra-thin silver foil which is edible. Rice is eaten accompanied by curries, *raita* (seasoned yogurt), chopped salad vegetables and also chutney—pickles. One of the varieties of chutneys is green chutney made of freshly ground coriander leaves, green chilies, salt and onion, with or without coconut and tamarind or lemon juice to make it sharp. Lemon, mango, coconut, and mint chutneys are a few of the other common varieties. Another accompaniment for rice which is very popular in the North regions is *papad;* this is made from processed wheat or lentil flour rolled into thin circular sheets served fried, or sometimes roasted. In the North it is usually spiced with black pepper and cumin seeds. It bloats up and becomes crisp like a wafer when fried in deep fat. Vegetarians prefer dishes such as *mattar panir* which is made from cottage cheese, diced and fried and then cooked with fresh peas.

North Indians partake of *dal* at almost every meal and usually round off the meal with a sweet dish such as *kheer* or *halwa* which has been previously described—or with *firnee,* a creamy rice pudding made of rice flour and milk. Any of the large varieties of fruits such as Kashmir apples, Kulu pears, pomegranates, guavas, tangerines, oranges, and grapes, may be preferred to sweets at the end of the meal.

For beverages the North Indians prefer tea or a cold beverage called *nimboo pani* (fresh lemon juice). Mango juice, tomato juice, pineapple juice, and grapefruit juice as well as *lassi*—yogurt beaten up, diluted with water, sweetened or salted—is also a popular Indian drink.

Before leaving our discussion of North Indian cookery it must be mentioned that in Kashmir boiled rice forms the staple food although it does not have that prominent a position in the rest of the region.

EAST INDIA

Bengal—the land of poets and artists—has a food tradition which clearly identifies it. Mustard oil is used as the cooking medium. Fish is a must for all meals. Food, on the whole, is plainer than in North India. Rice, especially boiled rice, is the staple of the diet and a popular wheat preparation called *loochi* made of refined wheat flour, clarified butter, and water made into a dough, rolled out into circles and deep-fried, is much loved. In other parts of India *loochi* is known as *poori* and is eaten as an accompaniment to a delicious potato delicacy called *dum aloo* which is sometimes stuffed with almonds and raisins and sometimes served with the addition of yogurt. Fried eggplant is also eaten with *loochi* as a first course. This is followed by a second course consisting of rice and *machher-jhol*, a soupy curry of vegetables and fish to which a little sugar or molasses has been added. Lentils and vegetables are also present on the menu. On special occasions, meat curry and rice are included. *Katti kebab*—meat pieces made tender by marinading them in spices, then barbecued on a skewer—is a favorite with the Anglo-Indian and Muslim population in Bengal.

Bengali sweets are well known all over India and are very varied. Most are milk sweets, such as: *sandesh*, *rasgulla*, and *gulab jamun*—the recipes for which may be found in this book.

SOUTH INDIA

South Indians are well known as rice eaters, and their food is very simple. The curries are generally hotter than those made in the North, but they are not as rich. Less fat is used, the cooking medium being gingili oil. Nonvegetarian curries of the mulligatawny (a word of Tamil derivation) type are made with chicken or mutton. Coconut milk is added to the curry to make a thinner gravy. *Sambar*, a preparation of vegetables with lentils and *rasam*, a spicy clear soup, are very popular as is *pachadi*, the counterpart of the North India *raita*. Different flavoring and seasoning are used in the yogurt however. South Indian desserts are made out of vermicelli or rice or lentils boiled in milk or coconut milk and sweetened with sugar or molasses. They are generally served at the end of the meal. South Indians love snacks and two of their favorites are *idli*—a mixture of ground lentils and rice, fermented and steamed in molds—and *masala dosa*—made crisp and paper thin and filled with potato. They are eaten with sweet or sour chutney as preferred.

The South Indian never refuses an offer of coffee, and for him, any time is coffeetime. The coffee in this region has a great reputation and most South Indian women take great pride in the preparation of coffee. The beans are roasted and fresh ground, then percolated. Almost all restaurants and hotels of the South serve an excellent brew.

In Cochin the food is exceedingly plain. Boiled rice is the staple food and the accompanying curries and vegetables have plenty of coconut in them making these dishes less hot than those prepared in Madras.

Sea and river foods are a specialty in this port as are a variety of fruits, the more popular being banana, pineapple, papaya, custard apple, and mango.

WEST INDIA

Bombay—the gateway of India—is a region with a very large range of delicacies exceedingly different from those found elsewhere. The nonvegetarian food in Bombay is influenced by the Parsees and Goans and the vegetarian food by the Gujaratis and Maharashtrians. *Dhan sak*, a Parsee dish is most popular. It is plain fried rice served with a curry called "wide mouthed" as it contains numberless ingredients among which are meats, lentils, vegetables, leafy vegetables, nuts, and spices. This dish is not hot tasting but some of the other Parsee preparations—*Bombay Duck*, a slim white fish served curried or fried, and *Patrani machhli*—are two such specialties.

Among the Goan preparations which are very sharp and tasty are *vindaloo*, a preparation of meat and spices marinated in vinegar into which the spices are ground, then cooked, and such other meat specialties as lamb chili-fry, lamb *indad* and "country captain." Goan vegetable preparations called *foogaths* are very pleasant and are generally made from coconut and vegetables which are not hot tasting. Cucumber with salad vegetables and onions chopped fine and mixed with a dash of lime juice and salt, forms the usual accompaniment for rice.

One of the special features of Maharashtrian and Gujarati food is that a sweet dish is served as the first course and is eaten with vegetables and *poori*, a wheat preparation resembling the Bengali *loochi*, but heavier in texture. A variety of fried foods are served with the meals, and the vegetables and lentils are slightly sweetened. The Maharashtrian starts the meal with rice and ends it with rice while the Gujarati eats the wheat preparations first and the rice last. On the whole it is important to note that much less rice is eaten here than in the South.

The most popular sweets are *shrikhand* (sweetened yogurt with all the liquid removed), *doodh pak* (rice pudding), *barfi* (a fudgelike sweet), and *jalebis* which are as pleasing to the eye as they are to the palate.

The specialties of Bombay sold by vendors all over the city are Bhel Puri and Khasta Kachuri, particularly on the famous Juhu and Chowpatty beaches.

Both coffee and tea, as well as lemon juice sweetened with sugar and bottled fruit juices, are considered extremely refreshing. *Neera*, a pleasant nonfermented drink taken from the coconut palm is available at all wayside restaurants and railway stations.

These short appetite-teasing descriptions of the various food interests in the different regions of India should be enough then to pique the curiosity and interest of the American who wants to become better acquainted with the foods of this newest of great democracies.

Centuries ago India's scholars taught the world the basic principles of grammar, phonetics, and mathematics. India invented the decimal system, the concept of zero, and the value of infinity. For our amusement India taught us chess, told us animal fables, and gave us the tales of the *Arabian Nights*.

Now, through this book, the women of India continue their generous tradition of sharing with American homemakers their secrets of spicery as perfected in curries and other Indian specialties.

Some Customs of the Indian Culinary Craft

What does one see as one walks past the door to an Indian kitchen? Burnished copper and brass, bright as if newly bought. These gleaming vessels are stacked one on top of another by a hand with a flair for interior decoration. One also sees the steady flame of the fire. Gadgets may be next to nil, the fireplace may be primitive, there may be no built-in shelves or a stove but always the meticulous care for brass and copper is evident. (Those who can afford it will engage a woman just for the purpose of polishing.) Why, one asks, this care? It is because of the flame which is lit in front of the family deity. The kitchen is the vital room in a Hindu household. It is the place of worship. It is also the dining room. There is where everyday family rites are held—never ceasing as is indicated by the flame. Nothing unclean may enter! No one may step in with shod feet. The vessels are kept shining so as to attract a god, and reflect the brightness of the constant flame.

The gadgets in an Indian kitchen may be cumbersome and antediluvian, but they are eminently suited to the jobs they must perform. For example, the rotary muller and heavy stone used for making rice or lentil paste is time consuming. Rice and lentils are soaked in the morning. In the evening the person who will do the grinding takes up the task. The stone may be built in the verandah outside the kitchen. First a mug of soaked lentils will be put in and the daughter of the house will roll the muller round and round with one hand, pushing in the rice with the other. In a few minutes the contents of the mug will increase. It must increase to about six times its original amount and become absolutely silky to the touch. The lentils must resemble the foam on a shaving brush. The daughter will not complain about this routine for she knows that tomorrow's breakfast will be good and the family will start another happy day.

The use of the cooking vessels may seem tedious to the modern homemaker but the traditions associated with it have come down through the centuries. In olden days baking was done in a pit similar to our modern-day barbecue arrangement. Either it was dug below ground or was a small, raised, brick oven-type contrivance with firm sides to reflect heat. It is called a *tandur*. Today it is not in great use; instead the everyday practice in almost all homes is the use of the *Dham-Pac*, for slow cooking. This heavy metal pan with a tight lid is essential, and it is similar to our own Dutch ovens or iron casseroles.

In the great tradition of Palav cooking, the dish containing the seasoned rice and meats becomes the oven as well, and its a better oven for this purpose than our up-to-date conveniences. A tight lid is put on the casserole, and the top and bottom are sealed together with dough. The casserole is then placed over gentle heat. A few hot coals are placed on top of the lid. The right dryness is thereby instilled to whatever is in the pot. Also this cooking method draws out the essences of the spices which have been placed in the liquid. In order to capture whatever droplets have formed on the lid, the dish is held with both hands and given a sharp tilt upward which pushes the rice against the upper lid and gathers up all the distilled flavors. Then the casserole is opened.

Another interesting cooking method is the use of a very hot ladle. First, butter is melted in the ladle and spices are added and cooked, then the entire thing, spoon and all is dashed into the vegetable. Since the spoon is iron and red hot it imparts a subtle, smoky flavor to the dish. In the American kitchen the same effect can be achieved by plunging a butter melter or soup ladle, in which the spices have been cooked, into vegetables such as cabbage, squash, or tomatoes.

This combination of texture and flavor is very important in the cooking of vegetables which have an important status of their own and are not considered merely as meat substitutes even though upon occasions they are used to give specific character to the gravy of the curries.

India's dining etiquette is very definite and is carried on in a prescribed way. The ritual of correct serving is instilled from childhood. At a private party the girls of the family serve the men and children; later the men serve the women. On these occasions servants are not allowed into the dining room which is held as a very special place.

For a large affair, dining table and chairs are stowed away. The inner courtyard is washed and cleaned, and rows and rows of low stools are arranged on which the guests sit cross-legged. Another row of stools, slightly higher, are placed in front of each setting. Upon this stool *thaali*—a large platter about ten inches in diameter with a one-inch ledge—is placed. If the occasion is a wedding feast for, say, fifty persons, long narrow mats are spread out for the guests to sit on, and plantain leaves take the place of the *thaali*. There is a correct way of laying the leaf or *thaali*. The tapering end of the leaf should be to the left of the diner (the plantain leaf generally averages about 18"×12" in size). A ceremonial meal should consist of fourteen different foods; eighteen is about the maximum. These are served in a definite pattern (see illustration), the items are numbered according to order of service and include:

1. Salt
2. Chutney
3. Pickles
4. Uncooked vegetable seasoned with curds, i.e., *pachadi*
5. Dry vegetable preparation or cutlet
6. *Dal* (chick-peas, yellow split peas, etc.) or curds
7. Rice spiced with vegetable or meat
8. *Papad*, potato or banana chips
9. The main curry and a *rasam* or soup
10. *Idli* or *masalah dosai*, a lentil dish
11. *Ladu* or *poli*, dessert
12. Payasam, a milk pudding
13. Rice, plain boiled
14. Ghee

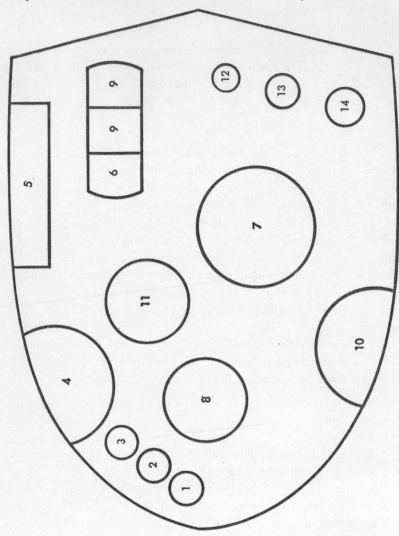

The small bowls holding foods numbered 1, 2, 3, 12, 13, and 14 are called *katoris*. Sometimes they are made from hardy leaves stuck together; sometimes they are brass, copper, silver, or gold, as are the *thaalis* upon which they rest.

Indian food is eaten with the fingers and is cooked specifically for this method although it is not taboo to lift the *katori* to drain off a gravy or sauce when it is too good to leave. At no time, at serving or eating (not even to break a *chapati*), may the left hand be used. Only the five fingers up to the second joints may be used. The palms of the hands should be kept clean at all times. When the feast is over a tumbler of water is served and is taken with the left hand. The hands and mouth are rinsed and all repair to the courtyard for the evening. After dinner, munches made of spices wrapped in betel leaf are passed. For a big party these come wrapped in betel leaves touched off with gold and sprinkled with rose water. Where caste distinctions prohibit a visitor from eating in a friend's home, they will offer each other a munch as a token of good will and it will be accepted in the same spirit.

In some households a little ritual is enacted every day before the food is distributed, best showing the spirit which pervades the serving and cooking of Indian cuisine.

The lady of the house says grace before meals. She pours some ghee into a *pooja* (prayer) spoon. After it has been thoroughly heated, it is used to stir into the curry. Then in token of inviting God as the chief guest, she claps her hands once, pronouncing the prayer which is a simple plea to bless the results of her routine work in preparing for her family. With this grace pronounced the meal is taken.

Thus we see the relationship and significance of the spiritual to food and its preparation . . . it is a spirit which invades all the delectable dishes of Indian cookery.

SPICE EQUIVALENTS

(Information provided by The American Spice Trade Association)

One-inch piece of ginger=1¼ teaspoon ground ginger
One-inch stick of cinnamon=1 teaspoon ground cinnamon
Two-inch whole dry pepper=1 teaspoon crushed red pepper
1 teaspoon whole cloves=¾ teaspoon ground cloves
1 teaspoon coriander seeds=1 teaspoon ground coriander
1 teaspoon mustard seeds=1½ ground mustard
1 teaspoon cumin seeds=1¼ teaspoons ground cumin
4 medium-size whole-pod cardamoms=½ teaspoon ground
 cardamom

Part I
CURRY

Introduction to Curry

The word CURRY is magic. Its mention conjures up for us the romance and mystery of the far-off land of the Taj Mahal. The pulse quickens to the thought of the exotic.

The best way to create the Indian atmosphere is to perfume your home with the essences of curry cooking. The exact origin of the word is not clear but its earliest precise mention dates back to about A.D. 477 in an Indian tale wherein one of the characters "partook of rice dressed in butter, with its full accompaniment of curries." This would not have been seasoned with curry powder, for even today culinary tradition in India demands that the housewife grind or bruise whole spices as they are needed for the day's meals. Curry, as a word, seems to have come into English usage about 1530, but even today in all regional languages "curry"— each different variety of hundreds—has its own specific name. Its meaning, no matter what the word, simply implies sauce—a richly spiced one to be sure. It can be thick, thin, or medium. It can enhance meat, fowl, fish, seafood, or vegetables and is always marvelously aromatic due to the mixture of many different spices.

In the main, a curry may be classed under any of these four groups:

1. *Those with a picklelike flavor*—cooked in spices such as cumin, mustard, paprika, turmeric, cinnamon, cloves, and poppy seeds.
2. *Stewy types*—coconut milk or paste is used to provide ample gravy. Coriander seeds, coriander leaf, ginger, garlic, and green chili are the condiments that flavor this.
3. *Vegetable in a sauce*—generally sour milk or diluted yogurt (by Indian standards this is a mild dish, for only a very little cumin, chili, garlic, and coconut are used).

4. *The lentil and gram curries*—the mainstay of the vegetarians —is peppery, faintly sweet, definitely sour, and exotic because of the tamarind.

But what is fascinating are the dozens and dozens of changes that are possible within the four classifications. *Korma* is a dry curry. The sauce clings to the cooked meat much as a barbecue sauce would. Meats used in a *korma* are marinated in yogurt before cooking and some cooks thicken the sauce by adding dried coconut or poppy seeds. Kebab curries, made up of meat, onions, ginger, garlic pieces, etc., are threaded on short skewers, then fried and simmered in spiced gravy. *Kofta* curries are made of finely ground chicken or mutton shaped into balls, then cooked slowly in a curry sauce. *Vindaloo* is a sour curry in which the meats are marinated in well-spiced vinegar for several hours before they are cooked.

If you've ever looked through the eye of a kaleidoscope and watched its myriad color groupings—ever changing in its small, rigid, confined area—you can understand the principle of creativity in curry cooking.

The basic method of the curry process is as follows:

1. FRY onions in hot fat
2. FRY sweet spices, i.e., cardamoms, cloves, cinnamon
3. FRY 1 tablespoon of curry powder
4. Two pounds of meat, fowl, fish, seafood, or vegetables according to taste
5. One cup coconut milk or tomato purée, for simmering

One notices here the words "curry powder." It is traditional that Indian cooks begin the preparation of each recipe by grinding or crushing whole spices, freshly ground for each meal. The sound of this spice pounding is said to be one of the most familiar sounds of India. But even in India cooks are likely to use a certain amount of curry powder as a sort of background seasoning. No two curry powders are the same in formula but all commercial curry powders are certain to include such spices as cayenne, coriander, cumin, fenugreek, and turmeric. They may also contain one or more spices such as allspice, cassia, cardamom, cloves, fennel, ginger, mace, yellow mustard, and black or white pepper.

Curry powder is such a great convenience that we might almost be misled into thinking this is a new invention. It isn't. It is probably the world's earliest spice blend. Seafaring men brought curry powder home from the Far East centuries ago as a treasure for wife or mother.

Before the early sixteenth century, curries and curry powders were made without capsicum peppers—the chilies the Indians love so much. When Columbus discovered America he also discovered many members of the great capsicum family—the pod peppers. Word of this spice spread as fast as ships could sail and within a decade capsicums were brought to India by the Portuguese. It was at this point that curries took on the character they have today. A curry dish without the snap of red peppers is unthinkable today and curry powder blended for Indian use includes a greater amount of capsicums than formulas we use here in our own country.

Curry powders used in Europe during the late Middle Ages probably were without turmeric, the root which gives curry powder its intense golden-yellow color, and there is evidence that saffron was used instead. Cumin seed is one of man's oldest aromatics. It is mentioned in the Bible. Coriander seed is another and even though we don't know it we eat a great deal of it since it is one of the principal seasonings of frankfurters. Fenugreek is a seed of the pea family. It is pleasantly bitter, with the flavor hinting of burnt sugar. It is of course obtainable in the United States and is the spice which gives curry its distinctive aroma—the one with which this delectable food is identified.

So here is a chance for the American cook to really "get into the act." Making curry gives plenty of room for individuality. The ideas you use depend upon the range of your spice shelf—if you don't cut down wildly on one spice or add drastically to another— every experiment can be a culinary masterpiece.

Take courage! Grind your own spices or open that container of curry powder—take a big, deep whiff—and LET YOURSELF GO! You will be following Indian footsteps to fabulous food.

SPECIAL HINTS

In curry recipes rhubarb has been used as a substitute for the authentic Indian ingredient, tamarind. In the making of chutneys, unripe mango, peeled, grated, or finely chopped before cooking, is used as the tamarind substitute. In every case, the white wine used in these recipes is a substitute for India toddy.

DO NOT use packaged, commercial sweet coconut in preparing any of the dishes in this book. Use ONLY fresh coconut or commercial unsweetened coconut. Fresh is best.

To make thick coconut milk: Soak for 1 hour in 1 cup of milk ½ cup of freshly grated coconut. Strain milk before using.

To make thin coconut milk: Soak for 1 hour in 2 cups of milk ½ cup of freshly grated coconut. Strain milk before using.

To make flour of split peas, lentils, chick-peas: Place them in an ungreased skillet in the oven. Brown well, shaking from time to time for five minutes. Pour into a high-speed blender. Pulverize and sift fine. Always make a little extra and keep in a tightly covered jar.

To make rice flour: Same method as above.

Curry Powder, Paste, and Sauce

CURRY POWDER I
[Masalah]

2 teaspoons chili powder
2½ teaspoons cumin seeds
3 tablespoons coriander seeds
¼ teaspoon mustard seeds
2 teaspoons ground turmeric
⅛ teaspoon fenugreek seeds

Place all ingredients in high-speed blender or spice grinder. Grind to a fine powder. Place in tightly covered jar. Medium-hot taste. *Yield* ¼ cup

CURRY POWDER II
[Masalah]

1 pound ground turmeric
¾ pound ground coriander
6 tablespoons ground ginger
4 tablespoons ground black
  pepper
3 tablespoons cayenne
3 tablespoons ground
  cardamom
1 tablespoon ground caraway
  seeds
3 teaspoons ground cloves
½ pound cumin seeds

Blend together all ingredients. Place in tightly covered jar. Medium-hot taste. *Yield* 2½ pounds

CURRY POWDER III
[*Masalah*]

2 *pounds coriander seeds*
½ *pound whole dry red*
peppers
1 *pound turmeric*

½ *pound cumin seeds*
½ *pound fenugreek seeds*
½ *pound black pepper*

Divide all spices into small portions. Place in high-speed blender or spice grinder. Grind to a powder. When all spices are reduced to powder, place in large mixing bowl. Mix together to blend ingredients perfectly. Place in tightly covered jars. Very hot taste. *Yield* 5 pounds

CURRY POWDER IV
[*Masalah*]

½ *pound ground coriander*
½ *teaspoon chili powder*
2 *tablespoons ground black*
pepper
9 *tablespoons ground cumin*

6 *tablespoons ground*
fenugreek
2 *tablespoons ground ginger*
1 *tablespoon ground poppy*
seeds

Blend together all ingredients. Place in tightly covered jar. Medium-hot taste. *Yield* approximately 1 pound

CALCUTTA CURRY MIX
[*Masalah*]

1 *tablespoon coriander seeds*
½ *tablespoon poppy seeds*
1 *one-inch turmeric stick*

½ *teaspoon ground ginger*
1 *teaspoon cumin seeds*
¼ *teaspoon chili powder*

Place all ingredients in high-speed blender or spice grinder. Grind to a fine powder. Place in tightly covered jar. Medium-hot taste. *Yield* ¼ cup

CURRY PASTE I
[Masalah]

16 tablespoons ground
   coriander
7½ teaspoons ground cumin
4 tablespoons ground turmeric
1 teaspoon chili powder
4 tablespoons peppercorns,
   ground
6 tablespoons ground mustard

7½ teaspoons ground ginger
2 tablespoons crushed garlic
6 tablespoons salt
8 tablespoons sugar
8 tablespoons split-pea flour
White vinegar
¼ cup salad oil

Blend all spices together in bowl. Add enough white vinegar to make mixture the consistency of thick jelly. Heat salad oil in skillet. Add spices. Fry, adding more oil if necessary, until mixture is reduced to a paste. Spoon into jar. Cover tightly when cool. Use in sandwiches or on fried bread or biscuits. Mild taste. *Yield* approximately 1½ cups

CURRY PASTE II
[Masalah]

1 tablespoon salad oil
2 tablespoons ground
   coriander
½ teaspoon chili powder
1¼ teaspoons ground cumin
¾ teaspoon ground mustard

1 teaspoon ground turmeric
1 teaspoon chopped garlic
1¼ teaspoons ground ginger
1 tablespoon lemon pulp
Water

Heat salad oil in skillet. Add all spices and lemon pulp. Fry 2 or 3 minutes, mixing with fork. Add enough water slowly to make spices the consistency of paste. Spoon into jar. Cover tightly when cool. Medium-hot taste. *Yield* ½ cup

MADRAS CURRY POWDER
[*Masalah*]

1½ pounds coriander seeds
¾ pound whole dry red
  peppers
4 tablespoons ground black
  pepper
⅓ pound cumin seeds

12 tablespoons ground
  turmeric
10 tablespoons fenugreek
  seeds
8 tablespoons mustard seeds

Place all ingredients in high-speed blender or spice grinder.
Grind to a powder. Blend well. Place in tightly covered jar. Medium-hot taste. *Yield* 3 pounds

CURRY SAUCE I
[*Masalah*]

2 tablespoons vegetable
  shortening
1 medium onion, thinly
  sliced
1 tablespoon curry powder

2 teaspoons flour
½ cup beef bouillon
½ cup milk
2 apple slices

Heat vegetable shortening in skillet. Add onions. Fry until soft,
not brown. Add curry powder, flour, bouillon, and milk. Simmer
for 5 minutes. Add apples if desired. Mild taste. *Yield* 1¼ cups
curry sauce

CURRY SAUCE II
[*Masalah*]

2 tablespoons vegetable
  shortening
1 small onion, finely sliced
1 medium carrot, finely sliced
1 teaspoon curry powder

1 tablespoon flour
4 slices of raw green apple
½ cup tomato sauce
2 cups beef bouillon

Heat vegetable shortening in skillet. Add onion and carrot. Fry until golden color, not brown. Combine curry powder and flour. Add a little water to make a smooth paste. Add paste to skillet. Add apple, tomato sauce, and bouillon. Simmer for ½ hour. Serve over hard-boiled eggs or cooked fish with hot rice. Mild taste. *Yield* 3 cups curry sauce

Lamb, Beef, and Chicken Curries

BAKED CHICKEN CURRY
[Chitamani]

1 small onion
1 teaspoon salt
¾ teaspoon ground turmeric
4 garlic cloves
1 teaspoon cayenne

2 tablespoons vinegar
3 pounds chicken parts,
    breast, thighs, legs
3 large onions, finely sliced
1 tablespoon brown sugar

Grind to a paste small onion, salt, turmeric, garlic, cayenne, and vinegar in food chopper. Use fine blade or high-speed blender. Rub chicken pieces with spice paste. Set aside for half hour. Place chicken in flat baking dish. Roast in 400° oven for 10 minutes. Remove. Cover with sliced onions. Cover baking dish tightly with foil. Return to 300° oven for 1 hour, or until chicken is tender. Sprinkle sugar over chicken. Return to oven uncovered for 5 minutes or until onions are lightly browned. Serve. Yield 8 to 10 servings

CHICKEN CURRY
[Moorgee Masalah]

8 chicken parts, breasts, legs
2 teaspoons ground coriander
1 teaspoon ground turmeric
4 garlic cloves, crushed
1½ teaspoons ground ginger
2 teaspoons salt
1 cup chopped onion
1 cup tomato purée
4 tablespoons vegetable
    shortening

2 teaspoons sesame seeds
1 teaspoon ground cardamom
¼ teaspoon ground
    cloves
1 teaspoon ground cinnamon
1 teaspoon cayenne
1 tablespoon poppy seeds,
    ground

Place chicken, coriander, turmeric, garlic, ginger, salt, onion, and tomato purée in large skillet. Cook slowly until onions are soft.

Curry

etable shortening in small skillet. Add
loves, cinnamon, cayenne, and poppy
. Turn into chicken skillet. Simmer
ximately 1 hour. *Yield* 6 to 8 servings

N IN LIME JUICE
orgee Tanjore]

½ cup lime juice	4 teaspoons ground cardamom
½ teaspoon salt	6 chicken breasts
1 teaspoon paprika	Vegetable oil
4 teaspoons ground coriander	

Combine lime juice, salt, paprika, coriander, and cardamom in
large mixing bowl. Make cuts across grain of chicken. Place chicken
in mixing bowl with lime juice and spices. Marinate for 1 hour.
Remove chicken and brush with oil. Place chicken in large skillet.
Pour marinade over chicken. Cover tightly. Cook until chicken is
tender, approximately 1 hour. *Yield* 6 servings

CHICKEN WITH POPPY SEEDS
[Moorgee Kurma]

5 tablespoons vegetable shortening, divided	Crushed red pepper to taste
4 medium onions, finely sliced	½ teaspoon ground ginger
8 cloves, crushed	1 tablespoon ground coriander
1 teaspoon ground cinnamon	2 cups hot water
¾ teaspoon ground ginger	½ coconut
1 teaspoon crushed garlic	1 tablespoon poppy seeds
1 cup yogurt	Salt to taste
1 broiler-fryer chicken, 2½ to 3½ pounds, cut up	24 cashew nuts
	Juice of 1 lime

Heat 4 tablespoons vegetable shortening in large skillet. Add onions and brown. Add separately—cloves, cinnamon, ¾ teaspoon ginger, and garlic. Add yogurt. Add chicken. Fry for 4 or 5 minutes. Heat 1 tablespoon vegetable shortening in small skillet. Add crushed red pepper, ½ teaspoon ginger, and coriander. Fry 2 or 3 minutes and add to chicken. Add hot water and cover tightly. Cook approximately 1 hour. Grind together to a fine paste the coconut, poppy seeds, and salt. Use fine blade of food chopper or high-speed blender. Add coconut paste to chicken when half cooked. Add nuts and lime juice. *Yield* 4 servings

CHICKEN ALMOND CURRY
[*Moorgee Badam*]

2 *broiler-fryers, 2½ to 3 pounds*	2 *tablespoons almonds, finely ground*
1½ *teaspoons ground ginger*	2 *tablespoons poppy seeds, finely ground*
1 *teaspoon salt*	
2 *teaspoons ground cinnamon*	2 *tablespoons slivered almonds*
1 *teaspoon paprika*	
Vegetable oil for frying	9 *whole cardamoms, crushed*
2 *medium onions, chopped*	1 *teaspoon saffron*
1 *cup tomato purée*	4 *tablespoons of lime juice*

Cut up chicken into parts. Rub ginger, salt, 1 teaspoon of cinnamon and paprika into chicken and set aside for half an hour. Fry chicken in oil. When evenly fried on all sides, add onions and cook until onions are very soft. Add tomato purée and simmer until chicken is cooked, approximately 1 hour. Add ground almonds and ground poppy seeds. In a separate small frying pan, add about 1 teaspoon of oil and gently fry slivered almonds, 1 teaspoon cinnamon and cardamom. Add to curry. Turn chicken curry into serving dish. Soak saffron in lime juice. Sprinkle curry with saffron and lime juice. *Yield* 8 to 10 servings

CHICKEN AND APRICOTS
[*Murgh Khoo Bani*]

1 broiler-fryer chicken, 2½ to
3 pounds
2 tablespoons vegetable
shortening
2 medium onions, finely
chopped
¼ teaspoon crushed garlic
½ teaspoon ground ginger
2 medium tomatoes, chopped
1 one-inch cinnamon stick
2 cardamoms
Salt to taste
1 cup dried apricots
¼ teaspoon saffron
¼ cup warm milk

Cut chicken in 8 pieces. Heat shortening in large skillet and fry onions until light brown. Add garlic and ginger, fry well. Add chicken, tomatoes, cinnamon, cardamoms, and salt. Add just enough water to half-cover chicken. Cover and simmer until chicken is almost cooked, approximately 1 hour. Add apricots. If necessary add just enough water to allow apricots to cook. Crush saffron in warm milk and add at the same time as apricots. Cover and cook until apricots are soft, not pulpy. *Yield* 4 to 5 servings

CHICKEN IN SPICES
[*Murgh Masalah*]

1 broiler-fryer chicken, 2½ to
3 pounds
1 large onion, quartered
1 one-inch piece of ginger
3 garlic cloves
1 teaspoon ground turmeric
1 teaspoon cumin seeds
1 two-inch cinnamon stick
2 cardamoms
4 cloves
5 large tomatoes, peeled and
chopped
2 cups boiling water
Butter or margarine
2 tablespoons vegetable
shortening

Cut chicken in 8 pieces. Grind together to paste in food chopper using fine blade or in high-speed blender the onion, ginger, garlic, turmeric, cumin, cinnamon, cardamoms, and cloves. In a large casserole place chicken, ground onion and spices, tomatoes and water. Dot with butter or margarine. Cover and simmer until chicken is tender, approximately 1 hour. Heat shortening in skillet. Add cooked chicken and fry for a few minutes. *Yield* 4 to 5 servings

CHICKEN AND POTATO CURRY
[*Murgeer Malai Masalah*]

5 tablespoons vegetable shortening, divided
4 medium potatoes, cubed
1 bay leaf
4 cloves
2 cardamoms
1 one-inch cinnamon stick
1 medium onion, finely sliced
1 medium onion, quartered
½ garlic clove
¾ teaspoon ground ginger
Crushed red peppers to taste
½ teaspoon ground turmeric
½ teaspoon chili powder
1 chicken, 2½ to 3½ pounds, cut in 8 pieces
Salt to taste
Sugar to taste
2 cups coconut milk

Heat 4 tablespoons vegetable shortening in casserole or Dutch oven. Add potatoes. Fry and reserve. In same casserole, add 1 tablespoon vegetable shortening, bay leaf, cloves, cardamoms, and cinnamon. Fry 2 or 3 minutes. Add sliced onions. Fry until brown. Place quartered onion, garlic, and ginger in food chopper. Use fine blade or high-speed blender. Grind to a paste. Add to fried onions. Fry 2 or 3 minutes. Add crushed red peppers, turmeric, chili powder, chicken, salt, and sugar. Fry 4 or 5 minutes. Turn chicken while frying. Add coconut milk. Cook until chicken is almost tender, approximately 1 hour. Add potatoes. Simmer until chicken and potatoes are done. (Shrimp may be substituted for chicken.) *Yield* 4 servings

STUFFED CHICKEN
[Murgh-Do-Pyaza]

¼ cup lemon pulp
Whole dry red or green
    pepper to taste
8 slivers of garlic
1 teaspoon cumin seeds
1 teaspoon mustard seeds
1 teaspoon coriander seeds
1 two-inch piece of ginger
Salt to taste
2 tablespoons vegetable
    shortening
Chicken giblets, chopped
1 chicken, 3 to 4 pounds
½ coconut
½ teaspoon ground
    coriander

1 one-inch piece of ginger,
    fresh or crystallized
6 slivers of garlic
3 cloves
½ teaspoon ground
    cardamom
Whole dry red or green
    pepper, chopped, to taste
1 teaspoon ground turmeric
Salt to taste
6 large onions, cut in thick
    slices
4 large potatoes, cut in thick
    slices
Butter or margarine

Place lemon pulp, pepper, garlic, cumin, mustard, coriander, ginger, and salt in food chopper using fine blade or in high-speed blender. Grind to a paste. Heat shortening and fry giblets and ground spices with lemon pulp. Fry for a few minutes, then stuff entire mixture into chicken; sew up opening. Place coconut, coriander, ginger, garlic, cloves, cardamom, pepper, turmeric, and salt in food chopper using fine blade or in high-speed blender. Grind to a paste. Rub some over chicken, and use the rest between onions and potatoes. Line the bottom of a casserole with dots of butter or margarine. Spread layer of onions over butter or margarine. Place in chicken. Surround with potatoes. Spread another layer of onions over potatoes and dot with more butter or margarine. Cover tightly and seal the edges with foil or dough. Cook on low heat until chicken is tender, approximately 1 hour. *Yield* 4 to 5 servings

SPICED CHICKEN SAUTEED IN YOGURT AND SAUCE
[*Murgh Korma*]

3 *pounds breasts and legs of chicken*
½ *cup yogurt*
2¾ *teaspoons salt*
¾ *cup dehydrated onion flakes*
½ *cup water*
½ *cup vegetable shortening*
6 *whole cloves*
4 *whole cardamoms, cracked*
6 *peppercorns*
1 *cinnamon stick, 2 inches long*

2 *bay leaves*
1 *teaspoon ground turmeric*
1 *tablespoon coriander*
1 *teaspoon ground cumin seeds*
½ *teaspoon ground ginger*
½ *teaspoon ground red pepper*
¾ *teaspoon garlic powder*
½ *cup tomato purée*
¾ *cup water*

Wash chicken and mix with yogurt and salt. Let marinate 1 hour. Combine onion flakes and the ½ cup water and let stand 8 minutes to soften or until all water is absorbed. Melt shortening. Add onion flakes to melted shortening and cook 15 minutes or until well browned. Tie cloves, cracked cardamoms, and peppercorns in a cheesecloth bag and add along with cinnamon, bay leaves, and turmeric. Stir and cook 5 minutes. Add chicken and cook 10 minutes, turning occasionally. Cover and continue cooking 30 minutes. Add remaining spices and cook 5 minutes. Add tomato purée and water. Cook 10 minutes or until sauce has thickened. If chicken is not brown enough, remove chicken from sauce and brown it in hot shortening in another pan. Return chicken to sauce and serve with rice. *Yield* 8 servings

CHICKEN LEGS
[*Moorgee*]

12 chicken legs, skin removed
½ cup lime juice, divided
4 tablespoons vegetable
    shortening
4 cloves
1 teaspoon fennel seeds
1 bay leaf
6 peppercorns
1 teaspoon ground ginger

6 garlic cloves, chopped
2 teaspoons ground coriander
1 teaspoon ground cardamom
1 teaspoon cayenne pepper
1 teaspoon salt
1 medium onion, finely
    sliced
¼ cup grated coconut
2 tablespoons poppy seeds

Place chicken legs in large bowl with ¼ cup lime juice. Marinate for ½ hour. Heat vegetable shortening in Dutch oven or casserole. Add cloves, fennel, bay leaf, and peppercorns. Fry 3 or 4 minutes. Add ginger and garlic. Fry 3 or 4 minutes. Add coriander, cardamom, cayenne, salt, and chicken legs. Fry chicken on all sides. Add onion. Pour in remaining lime juice and juice from marinade. Cover. Cook slowly until chicken is tender, approximately 1 hour. Grind coconut and poppy seeds to a paste in food chopper. Use fine blade or high-speed blender. Stir paste in with chicken legs. Cook uncovered for 10 minutes. Serve. *Yield* 6 servings

SPICED CHICKEN SIMMER
[*Shahi Murgh*]

1 chicken, 3 to 4 pounds
2 tablespoons vegetable
    shortening
3 medium onions, sliced
¼ teaspoon ground ginger

Whole dry red or green
    pepper, chopped, to taste
Peppercorns to taste
Salt to taste
1 cup hot water

Cut or chop chicken in 12 or 14 pieces (cleaver is excellent for this). Heat shortening in skillet and fry onions until brown. Set aside and keep warm. In same skillet add pieces of chicken and fry until partially done. Add more shortening if necessary. Add ginger, pepper, peppercorns, and salt. Fry a few minutes more. Add 1 cup water and let chicken simmer until tender, approximately 1 hour. Serve with browned onions sprinkled over. *Yield* 4 to 5 servings

CHICKEN OR BEEF LIVER
[*Bhuni Kaleji*]

1 *medium onion, chopped*	*Salt to taste*
¾ *teaspoon ground ginger*	1 *tablespoon vinegar*
½ *garlic clove*	1 *pound chicken or beef*
Crushed red pepper to taste	*liver, cut in ½-inch slices*
½ *teaspoon ground turmeric*	1 *tablespoon vegetable*
Chili powder to taste	*shortening*
Ground black pepper to taste	1 *tablespoon lemon pulp*

Grind together onion, ginger, garlic, crushed red pepper, turmeric, chili powder, pepper, salt, and vinegar. Use food-chopper fine blade, or high-speed blender. Rub ground onion and spices into liver pieces. Heat vegetable shortening in skillet. Fry liver for 2 or 3 minutes. Add lemon pulp and salt. Fry until done. *Yield* 4 servings

STUFFED CHICKEN
[*Barela Murg*]

1½ *tablespoons vegetable*	1 *tablespoon yogurt*
shortening	½ *teaspoon ground turmeric*
¼ *cup chopped onions*	¾ *teaspoon allspice*
Giblets from chicken, chopped	½ *teaspoon paprika*
½ *cup ground beef*	2 *garlic cloves, crushed*
½ *cup cooked rice*	2 *tablespoons ground ginger*
1 *tablespoon raisins*	¼ *tablespoon ground*
1 *teaspoon salt, divided*	*cinnamon*
½ *tablespoon saffron, soaked*	¼ *tablespoon ground*
in 1 tablespoon warm water	*cardamom*
2 *tablespoons chopped parsley*	*Vegetable oil*
4-*pound roasting chicken*	

Heat vegetable shortening in skillet. Add onions. Fry until soft. Add giblets. Fry 2 or 3 minutes. Add ground beef, rice, raisins, ½ teaspoon salt, saffron, and parsley. Simmer 4 or 5 minutes. Fill cavity of chicken with giblet mixture. Sew up cavity. Combine yogurt, turmeric, allspice, paprika, garlic, ginger, cinnamon, cardamom, and ½ teaspoon salt. Rub spiced yogurt all over chicken. Set aside for 1 hour. Brush chicken with vegetable oil. Place in roasting pan. Cover with foil. Roast in 350° oven for 2½ hours. Remove foil. Roast for 15 minutes or until skin is crisp. *Yield* 8 to 10 servings

CHICKEN AND SPICES
[*Kanauji Mince*]

4-pound stewing chicken
4 cups boiling water
1 tablespoon saffron
1 tablespoon butter or margarine
½ tablespoon ground coriander
½ tablespoon onion powder
4 cloves

1 one-inch cinnamon stick
1 tablespoon salt
½ cup chopped onion
½ tablespoon ground cumin
½ tablespoon fennel seeds
2 garlic cloves
½ tablespoon paprika
1½ teaspoons ground ginger
1 medium onion, finely sliced

Place chicken, water, saffron, butter or margarine, coriander, onion, cloves, cinnamon, and salt in large kettle. Cook 2½ to 3 hours or until chicken is tender. Remove meat from bones in large pieces. Reserve stock. Place in food chopper: chopped onions, cumin, fennel, garlic, paprika, and ginger. Use fine blade or high-speed blender. Grind to a paste. Heat vegetable shortening in Dutch oven or casserole. Add sliced onions. Fry until brown. Add spice paste. Fry 3 or 4 minutes. Add chicken pieces. Fry until brown. Add ½ cup chicken stock. Simmer until all liquid is absorbed. Serve. *Yield* 6 to 8 servings

MULLIGATAWNY SOUP
[*Mulligatawny Shorba*]

6 to 8 pounds chicken backs
and necks
4 cups water
½ cup sliced carrots
2 tablespoons instant minced
onion
½ cup chopped celery
2 tablespoons parsley flakes
½ cup chopped mushroom
stems

4 tablespoons instant minced
onion
¼ cup water
2 tablespoons vegetable
shortening
4 teaspoons flour
1 tablespoon curry powder
4 teaspoons salt
½ cup heavy cream
¾ cup cooked rice

Combine first 7 ingredients, cover and cook until chicken is tender, approximately 2 hours. Remove chicken. Soften the 4 tablespoons instant minced onion in ¼ cup water. Brown in 2 tablespoons vegetable shortening. Stir in flour, curry powder, and salt. Gradually add chicken stock and cook for 7 to 8 minutes. Rub through a fine sieve. Stir in heavy cream. Heat thoroughly (do not boil). Serve with 2 tablespoons rice in each bowl. If desired, pick a little of the chicken from the bones and add a few pieces to each serving. *Yield* 6 servings

DUCK AND VEGETABLES
[*Pondicherry Budhuk Buffado*]

1 duck, 4 to 5 pounds
2 pounds cabbage, quartered
6 medium onions, quartered
4 whole dry green or red
peppers, seeded (optional)
2 teaspoons ground turmeric

8 garlic cloves, finely minced
1 teaspoon ground ginger
2 cups white wine
2 teaspoons brown sugar
2 teaspoons vinegar

Cut duck into 8 pieces or use cleaver. Place duck, cabbage, and onions in large casserole. Sprinkle duck with peppers, turmeric,

garlic, and ginger. Pour wine over duck and cover. Place in a 350°
oven for 1 hour. Remove casserole and pour or skim off excess fat.
Be careful not to lose all of the liquid. Add brown sugar and vinegar. Return duck to oven without cover for 1 to 1½ hours or until
the top of duck and vegetables are brown and very little gravy re-
mains. *Yield* 4 to 5 servings

BEEF ROAST
[Smore]

1 teaspoon cayenne	½ teaspoon ground turmeric
1 teaspoon ground cumin	Salt to taste
6 garlic cloves, crushed	4 pounds beef for roasting
¾ teaspoon ground ginger	2 cups boiling water
1 teaspoon ground cinnamon	1 tablespoon vegetable
1 bay leaf, crushed	shortening
2 teaspoons ground coriander	1 medium onion, finely
Juice of 1 lemon	sliced
2 tablespoons vinegar	

Combine all ingredients except meat, shortening, onions, and water. Mix to a paste. Prick meat all over with fork or skewer. Rub
meat with spice paste. Set aside for 2 hours. Place meat in Dutch
oven. Add boiling water. Cover tightly. Roast in slow oven 275°
for 3 hours. Remove meat and slice. Reserve the gravy. Melt
vegetable shortening in large skillet. Add onions. Fry until crisp.
Add meat slices. Cover with reserved gravy. Simmer for 5 minutes.
Serve. *Yield* 8 to 10 servings

POT ROAST
[Chilly Fry]

2 tablespoons vegetable	½ teaspoon cayenne
shortening	1 teaspoon ground coriander
1 large onion, finely sliced	2 pounds beef, cubed
4 garlic cloves, finely chopped	1 tablespoon lemon pulp
1 teaspoon ground cumin	Salt to taste
½ teaspoon ground ginger	

Heat vegetable shortening in large skillet or Dutch oven. Add onion and garlic. Fry for 2 or 3 minutes. Add cumin, ginger, cayenne, and coriander. Fry 2 or 3 minutes. Add meat and brown. Add enough hot water to barely cover meat. Add lemon pulp and salt. Cover. Simmer until meat is tender, approximately 1½ hours. *Yield* 4 servings

BEEF CURRY
[*Moghlai Qorma*]

3 *tablespoons vegetable shortening*
3 *medium onions, thinly sliced*
4 *slivers of garlic*
½ *teaspoon ground ginger*
A *few mint leaves*
½ *teaspoon ground cardamom*
⅛ *teaspoon ground cinnamon*
4 *peppercorns*

1 *teaspoon ground cumin*
Chili powder to taste
Salt to taste
1 *pound beef or lamb, small cubes*
2 *cups yogurt*
½ *teaspoon saffron*
¼ *cup warm milk*
1 *tablespoon blanched almonds, halved*
1 *tablespoon raisins*

Heat shortening in large skillet. Add onions and fry until light brown. Add garlic, ginger, mint, cardamom, cinnamon, peppercorns, cumin, chili powder, and salt. Fry for 5 minutes. Add meat and brown. Add yogurt a spoonful at a time, stirring until all yogurt is used. Cover tightly. Cook until meat is tender, approximately 1 hour. Crush saffron in milk. In small skillet lightly brown almonds and raisins. Add saffron, almonds, and raisins to meat just before serving. *Yield* 4 to 5 servings

MEATBALLS AND GREEN-PEA CURRY
[*Kawab–Mutter Masalah*]

MEATBALLS:

1 *pound chuck, ground*   ½ *teaspoon cloves*
1 *teaspoon garlic salt*   ¼ *teaspoon salt*
1 *teaspoon ginger*   1 *egg*
1 *teaspoon cinnamon*

SAUCE:

½ *onion, sliced*   1 *teaspoon anise, ground*
2 *tablespoons vegetable*   1 *teaspoon cinnamon*
  shortening   1 *teaspoon red pepper*
1½ *tablespoons coriander,*   ½ *teaspoon cloves*
  ground   *Salt*
2 *teaspoons turmeric*   4 *cups milk*
1 *teaspoon garlic salt*   2 *cups peas, cooked*
1 *teaspoon ginger*   2 *teaspoons vinegar*

Combine chuck and next 6 ingredients. Mix lightly but well. Shape
into 1-inch balls. Set aside. Sauté onion in shortening in large skillet until onion is soft. Add next 9 ingredients; mix. Cook over low
heat for 2 minutes. Add milk. Cover. Simmer for 5 minutes. Add
meatballs. Simmer, covered, for 10 minutes. Add peas; cook, uncovered, for 3 minutes. Remove from heat. Stir in vinegar. Serve
with Orange Rice (see Index). *Yield* 4 servings

BEEF CREAMY CURRY
[*Malai Masalah*]

½ cup vegetable oil, divided
½ teaspoon cayenne or red pepper
1 teaspoon ground turmeric
3 garlic cloves, chopped
1 half-inch piece fresh ginger, chopped
1 two-inch cinnamon stick
¼ cup sliced onions
2 pounds beef, cubed

4 cups thin coconut milk
1 cup thick coconut milk
1 tablespoon lemon pulp
1 teaspoon ground cardamom
½ teaspoon ground cloves
½ teaspoon ground ginger
Juice of 1 lime
4 slivers of garlic
½ teaspoon ground ginger
½ cup chopped onions

Place ¼ cup oil in skillet and add cayenne, turmeric, chopped garlic, fresh ginger, cinnamon, and onions. Fry spices and onions for a few minutes or until onions are soft. Place beef and thin coconut milk in large casserole and add fried onions and spices. Tightly cover and cook slowly until meat is tender and stock is reduced to 2 cups, approximately 1½ hours. Add thick coconut milk, lemon pulp, cardamom, cloves, ground ginger, and lime juice. Simmer curry for 15 minutes without cover. In a small skillet heat ¼ cup of oil and add slivered garlic, ground ginger, and chopped onions. Fry for a few minutes and add to curry. Pour some gravy into skillet, heat for a few minutes and pour back into curry. *Yield* 4 to 6 servings

BEEF BALLS AND GRAVY
[*Kofta Kheer Pyaza*]

2 *pounds ground beef*
Salt to taste
½ *tablespoon ground black*
  pepper
6 *thyme leaves*
1 *tablespoon ground*
  cardamom
4 *tablespoons vegetable*
  shortening

1 *small onion, finely sliced*
1 *teaspoon ground cinnamon*
4 *cloves*
4 *cups milk*
½ *cup cream*
½ *tablespoon ground nutmeg*

Combine ground beef, salt, pepper, thyme, and cardamom in large bowl. Blend well. Dip hands in milk. Make tiny meatballs. Heat vegetable shortening in large skillet. Add meatballs. Fry until brown. Add onions on top of meatballs. Add cinnamon and cloves. Cover. Cook until onions are soft. Stir. Add milk. Simmer until gravy is thick. Add cream and nutmeg. Serve. *Yield* 6 to 8 servings

CURRY SOUP
[*Gol Gumbaz*]

1 *pound finely ground beef*
1½ *teaspoons salt, divided*
1 *bay leaf, crushed*
2 *teaspoons fresh ground*
  pepper, divided
⅛ *teaspoon ground mace*
⅛ *teaspoon ground cloves*
½ *teaspoon ground cinnamon*
2 *cups yogurt*

1 *cup flour*
2 *cups tomato juice*
2 *tablespoons vegetable*
  shortening
1 *teaspoon ground ginger*
½ *teaspoon crushed garlic*
1 *cup grated onion*
3 *cups coconut milk*

Place meat, ¾ teaspoon salt, bay leaf, 1 teaspoon pepper, mace, cloves, and cinnamon in mixing bowl. Knead together until well mixed. Wet hands with yogurt. Divide meat into small marbles. Combine ¾ teaspoon salt, 1 teaspoon pepper, and 1 cup of flour. Spread out on flat dish. Spread yogurt on flat dish. Roll meat in flour, then yogurt, and then flour again. Be sure meat is well coated each time. Pour tomato juice in skillet. Heat. Add meatballs. Simmer 10 minutes. Heat vegetable shortening in Dutch oven or casserole. Add ginger and garlic. Fry 2 or 3 minutes. Add onions. Fry 2 or 3 minutes. Add coconut milk. Simmer. Add meatballs with tomato gravy. Simmer 5 minutes. *Yield* 4 to 6 servings

LAMB IN COCONUT MILK
[*Kuzhambu*]

2 *tablespoons vegetable shortening*	1 *tablespoon poppy seeds, ground*
1 *medium onion, finely sliced*	2 *pounds lamb, cubed*
1 *teaspoon paprika*	2 *cups thin coconut milk*
2 *teaspoons ground coriander*	1 *cup thick coconut milk*
1 *teaspoon ground cumin*	¼ *cup chopped parsley*
½ *teaspoon ground turmeric*	1 *teaspoon ground cardamom*
½ *teaspoon ground black pepper*	¼ *cup lemon juice*

Heat vegetable shortening in Dutch oven or casserole. Add onions. Fry until soft. Remove ¾ of onion. Fry remaining onions crisp. Add paprika, coriander, cumin, turmeric, pepper, and poppy seeds. Fry 3 or 4 minutes. Add meat. Fry until browned on all sides. Add thin coconut milk. Reduce heat. Cover. Simmer until meat is half cooked, approximately ½ hour. Add thick coconut milk. Simmer uncovered until meat is tender. Remove from heat. Add parsley, cardamom, and lemon juice. Cover. Serve. *Yield* 6 to 8 servings

MARINATED LAMB
[*Kaliya*]

2 *cups yogurt*
1 *teaspoon salt*
1 *tablespoon ground coriander*
1 *teaspoon ground black pepper*
2 *tablespoons grated coconut*
4 *pounds lamb, cut in large cubes*

3 *tablespoons vegetable shortening*
1 *one-inch cinnamon stick*
1 *teaspoon fennel*
4 *garlic cloves*
4 *cloves*
2 *large onions, finely chopped*

Place yogurt in large bowl with salt, coriander, pepper, and coconut. Beat well. Add meat. Marinate for 2 to 4 hours, the longer the better. Heat vegetable shortening in Dutch oven or casserole. Add cinnamon, fennel, garlic, and cloves. Fry 3 or 4 minutes. Add meat. Brown on all sides. Add onions. Cover. Simmer until onions are soft. Add yogurt that meat marinated in. Mix well. Simmer until meat is tender, approximately 2 hours. *Yield* 10 to 12 servings

SAFFRON LAMB
[*Kashmiri Salna*]

3 *tablespoons vegetable shortening*
2 *pounds lamb, cubed*
½ *cup yogurt*
1 *teaspoon ground cumin*
½ *teaspoon ground ginger*

½ *teaspoon caraway seeds*
1 *teaspoon paprika*
Salt to taste
1 *teaspoon allspice*
1 *teaspoon saffron, soaked in* 1 *tablespoon water*

Heat vegetable shortening in Dutch oven or casserole. Add meat. Brown on all sides. Add yogurt. Simmer until yogurt is absorbed. Add cumin, ginger, caraway, paprika, salt, and allspice. Mix well. Sprinkle with hot water to make thick gravy. Cover. Simmer until meat is tender, approximately 1 hour. Sprinkle saffron water over meat. Cover. Remove from heat. Serve. *Yield* 6 to 8 servings

LAMB AND COCONUT MILK
[*Asaathu*]

2 *pounds lamb bones, cracked*
1 *cup chopped onions, divided*
1 *whole red pepper, split*
1 *two-inch cinnamon stick*
3 *cardamoms, crushed*
6 *cloves, divided*
1 *quart water*
3 *tablespoons vegetable shortening*
¾ *teaspoon ground turmeric*
1 *teaspoon ground ginger*
2 *garlic cloves, crushed*
2 *pounds lamb, cubed*
2 *tablespoons poppy seeds*
2 *tablespoons grated coconut*
½ *tablespoon ground marjoram*
Salt to taste
2 *cups coconut milk*
¼ *cup lime juice*

Place lamb bones, ½ cup onions, whole red pepper, cinnamon, cardamoms, cloves, and water in pan. Cook slowly for 1½ hours. Skim, strain, and reserve 1 cup of stock and marrow from bones. Heat vegetable shortening in large skillet. Add turmeric, ginger, and garlic. Fry 2 or 3 minutes. Add remaining onions. Fry until onions are soft. Add lamb. Fry 3 or 4 minutes. Grind together poppy seeds, coconut, marjoram, and salt, in food chopper using fine blade or high-speed blender. Combine with coconut milk and lime juice in small bowl. Add to meat. Add reserved stock and salt to taste. Cover. Simmer until meat is tender, stirring occasionally, approximately 1 hour. *Yield* 8 to 10 servings

LAMB AND YOGURT
[*Hyderabadi Goshth*]

4 *pounds boneless leg of lamb, fat trimmed*
1 *teaspoon ground turmeric*
1 *cup yogurt*
2 *teaspoons salt*
2 *teaspoons ground coriander*
3 *tablespoons vegetable shortening*
3 *half-inch cinnamon sticks*
½ *teaspoon ground cardamom*
8 *cloves*
8 *peppercorns*
1 *medium onion, finely sliced*
8 *garlic cloves, sliced*
¾ *teaspoon ground ginger*

Place meat, turmeric, yogurt, salt, and coriander in large bowl. Mix well. Set aside for 2 hours. Heat vegetable shortening in Dutch oven or casserole. Add cinnamon, cardamom, cloves, and pepper-corns. Fry 2 minutes. Add meat and yogurt. Simmer for 10 minutes. Add onions, garlic, and ginger. Cover. Simmer until meat is tender, approximately 2 hours. Serve. *Yield* 6 to 8 servings

POTTED LAMB
[*Ortakari*]

2 *pounds lamb, cut from leg, cubed*
2 *pounds breast of lamb, cubed*
4 *tablespoons lemon juice*
Salt to taste
½ *teaspoon cayenne*
2 *teaspoons ground coriander*
1 *large onion*
½ *cup grated coconut*
2 *tablespoons vegetable shortening*
4 *garlic cloves, crushed*
½ *cup chopped onion*
4 *bay leaves*
½ *cup chopped bell pepper*
1 *cup water*

Place meat, lemon juice, and salt in Dutch oven. Cover. Simmer 1 hour or until meat is half cooked. Skim off fat. Grind together to a paste: cayenne, coriander, large onion, and coconut in food chopper. Use fine blade or high-speed blender. Heat vegetable shortening in skillet. Add garlic, chopped onion, bay leaves and pepper. Fry 2 or 3 minutes. Add spice paste. Fry 5 to 10 minutes. Add to meat. Mix well. Add water to skillet spices were fried in. Bring to boil. Add to meat. Cover. Cook meat until tender, approximately 1 hour. *Yield* 8 to 10 servings

LAMB PEPPER WATER
[*Kari Rasam*]

4 *pounds breast of lamb, cubed*
¼ *teaspoon fenugreek, ground*
1 *teaspoon ground turmeric*
1 *teaspoon ground cinnamon*
2 *teaspoons ground coriander*
1 *teaspoon ground cumin*
1 *tablespoon lentils*
2 *cups chopped onion*
2 *teaspoons salt*
¼ *teaspoon crushed cloves*
½ *teaspoon cayenne*
1 *teaspoon freshly ground black pepper*
4 *garlic cloves*
Juice of ½ *lime*

Place lamb in large kettle. Add water to cover 6 inches above meat. Add fenugreek, turmeric, cinnamon, coriander, cumin, lentils, onion, and salt. Cook for 1 hour and 15 minutes or until meat is very tender. Skim off fat. Add cloves, cayenne, pepper, and garlic. Stir. Add lime juice. Serve boiled rice as accompaniment. *Yield* 8 to 10 servings

LAMB AND SUMMER SQUASH
[*Peerkangai Kari*]

½ *teaspoon cayenne*	1 *one-inch cinnamon stick*
¾ *teaspoon ground turmeric*	4 *cloves*
Salt to taste	6 *garlic cloves, crushed*
¾ *teaspoon ground cardamom*	2 *pounds lamb, cut from leg,*
1 *teaspoon ground ginger*	*cubed*
2 *tablespoons vegetable*	1 *small onion, finely sliced*
shortening	2 *cups diced summer squash*

Combine cayenne, turmeric, salt, cardamom, and ginger. Sprinkle over meat. Heat vegetable shortening in large skillet. Add cinnamon, cloves, and garlic. Fry for 1 or 2 minutes. Add meat. Fry until well browned. Add onion. Fry slowly until onions are soft. Add squash. Add small amounts of boiling water until meat is tender and squash is soft, approximately 1 hour. Serve. *Yield* 4 to 6 servings

LAMB CASSEROLE
[*Subh Degh*]

4 *tablespoons vegetable*	¾ *teaspoon turmeric*
shortening	1 *tablespoon chopped onions*
1 *medium onion, finely sliced*	1 *tablespoon ground coriander*
1 *pound ground lamb, rolled*	3 *small turnips, quartered*
in balls	3 *small carrots, sliced*
1 *pound lamb, cut in cubes*	2 *small squash, sliced in large*
2 *cups yogurt*	*pieces*
1 *tablespoon tomato purée*	

Heat vegetable shortening in Dutch oven or casserole. Add sliced onions. Fry 2 or 3 minutes. Add meatballs. Fry 2 or 3 minutes.

Add meat cubes. Fry 2 or 3 minutes. Combine yogurt, tomato purée, turmeric, chopped onions, and coriander. Add to meat. Mix well. Cover. Cook until meat is tender, approximately 1 hour. Remove cover. Cook until gravy is reduced to half. Add vegetables on top. Cover. Simmer for ½ hour or until vegetables are cooked. Serve. *Yield* 8 servings

LAMB CASSEROLE
[*Salna-Udaipuri*]

2 *pounds lamb, cubed*
Salt to taste
2 *cups chopped onions*
1 *bay leaf*
¼ *cup vegetable shortening*

2 *tablespoons ground
  coriander*
½ *teaspoon ground ginger*
1 *teaspoon allspice*
½ *teaspoon cayenne*
½ *cup yogurt, beaten*

Place meat, salt, onions, bay leaf and shortening in Dutch oven or casserole. Cover. Place in 350° oven until onions are soft. Heat large skillet. Add all ingredients from casserole. Fry for 5 minutes. Add following spices one at a time. Fry each spice 2 minutes. Do not change order: coriander, ginger, allspice, and cayenne. Add yogurt. Simmer until meat is tender, approximately 1 hour. *Yield* 6 to 8 servings

SILK-WEAVERS' MEAT

4 *pounds lamb, cut from leg,
  cubed*
1 *cup yogurt*
½ *cup grated onions*
4 *cups water*
4 *chicken bouillon cubes*
8 *garlic cloves, crushed*
¾ *teaspoon ground ginger*
½ *teaspoon ground black
  pepper*

1 *teaspoon ground cinnamon*
1 *teaspoon ground coriander*
¼ *cup ground coconut*
3 *tablespoons vegetable
  shortening*
1 *medium onion, finely sliced*
2 *teaspoons fennel seed*
1 *tablespoon chopped parsley*
Juice of 1 lime

Place meat in large bowl with yogurt and grated onions. Mix well. Set aside for 1 hour. Pour water in large pan. Add bouillon cubes, garlic, ginger, pepper, cinnamon, coriander, and coconut. Bring to a boil. Lower heat to allow bouillon to simmer. Heat vegetable shortening in large skillet or Dutch oven. Add sliced onions and fennel. Fry until crisp. Add meat, yogurt, and grated onions. Fry until meat separates from yogurt, about 10 to 15 minutes. Add bouillon. Cover. Simmer until gravy is reduced to half and meat is tender, approximately 2 hours. Serve in shallow dish. Sprinkle parsley and lime juice. *Yield* 10 to 12 servings

LAMB CURRY
[Indad]

2 *large onions*
1 *one-inch piece preserved*
  ginger, finely chopped
3 *garlic cloves, finely chopped*
¼ *cup white wine*
2 *tablespoons vegetable*
  shortening

2 *pounds lamb, cut in large*
  cubes
½ *teaspoon powdered cloves*
1 *teaspoon paprika*
2 *teaspoons salt*

Place onions in hot oven. Bake until soft. Mash onions. Combine ginger, garlic, and wine. Reserve. Heat vegetable shortening in large skillet until smoking hot. Add lamb and brown on all sides. Sprinkle cloves, paprika, and salt over meat. Stir meat to disperse flavors. Add mashed onions. Cover tightly and simmer. Remove cover when steam starts through cover. Stir in wine-and-spice mixture. Cover. Cook slowly until lamb is tender. *Yield* 4 servings

POTTED LAMB
[*Milagu Masalah*]

2 tablespoons peppercorns, crushed

½ tablespoon ground mustard seeds

½ teaspoon ground cinnamon

Salt to taste

1½ pounds leg of lamb, thinly sliced

½ cup vegetable shortening

2 medium onions, quartered

2 medium potatoes, sliced

2 cups hot chicken bouillon

Combine ground peppercorns, mustard, cinnamon, and salt in large mixing bowl with a little water to form a paste. Mix well. Rub meat with spices. Reserve for ½ hour. Heat vegetable shortening in large skillet. Place onions and meat in skillet. Cover meat with potatoes. Sprinkle with salt. Pour bouillon over meat and potatoes. Simmer until lamb is tender, approximately 1½ hours. *Yield* 4 servings

LAMB AND PEAS
[*Pattani Kari Kuzhambu*]

2 tablespoons vegetable shortening

1 pound lamb, cut in cubes

2 large onions, finely chopped

1 teaspoon ground turmeric

Salt to taste

1 one-inch cinnamon stick, broken in small pieces

4 cardamoms, crushed

1 tablespoon ground coriander

Crushed red pepper to taste

2 cups half-cooked peas

¼ coconut, grated

½ cup water

Heat vegetable shortening in large skillet. Add lamb, onions, turmeric, and salt. Cover and cook until meat is nearly done, approximately ½ hour. Add cinnamon, cardamoms, coriander, and crushed red pepper; mix well. Fry for 2 or 3 minutes. Add peas; combine coconut and water. Add to meat. Cook meat and peas until done. *Yield* 4 servings

MINCEMEAT PIES
[Mangsher Kochuri]

2 tablespoons vegetable
   shortening, divided
1 large onion, finely sliced
¾ teaspoon ground ginger
½ garlic clove, crushed
Crushed red peppers to taste
1 bay leaf
2 cloves

½ pound ground lamb
Salt to taste
1 teaspoon sugar
1½ tablespoons vinegar
1 cup all-purpose flour
⅛ teaspoon baking powder
Vegetable shortening for deep
   frying

Heat 1 tablespoon vegetable shortening in skillet. Add onion. Fry until brown. Add ginger, garlic, crushed red peppers, bay leaf, cloves, and meat. Fry 3 minutes. Add salt and sugar. Fry until meat is done. Add vinegar. Fry for 1 minute. Remove and allow to cool. Remove cloves and bay leaf. Sift together flour, salt, and baking powder. Rub in 1 tablespoon vegetable shortening. Knead well, adding enough water to make a soft dough. Divide into 8 balls. Roll out into pancake shape. In center of each, place a teaspoon of meat mixture. Fold each *kochuri* into half, forming semicircle. Seal edges well. Heat vegetable shortening in large skillet for deep frying. Fry *kochuri* till light brown. Yield 8 *kochuri*

LAMB AND POTATOES
[Maansha]

2 pounds lamb, cut from leg,
   cubed
½ cup tomato purée
1 teaspoon curry powder
4 tablespoons vegetable
   shortening
1 large onion, finely sliced
6 garlic cloves, crushed

¾ teaspoon ground ginger
¼ teaspoon cayenne
½ bay leaf
2 cloves
¼ teaspoon ground
   cardamom
2 cups fried potatoes

Place meat, tomato purée, and curry powder in large bowl. Mix well. Set aside for 2 hours. Heat vegetable shortening in Dutch oven or casserole. Add onions, garlic, ginger, cayenne, bay leaf, cloves, and cardamom. Fry for 4 or 5 minutes. Add meat. Fry until meat begins to stick. Add tomato purée that meat was marinated in. Add enough boiling water so that meat is covered. Simmer until meat is tender, approximately 1 hour. Place fried potatoes on meat. Cover. Cook 10 minutes. Serve. *Yield* 4 to 6 servings

LAMB CURRY
[*Thayir Masalah*]

½ teaspoon ground turmeric
1 teaspoon ground coriander
Crushed red peppers to taste
1 garlic clove, crushed
½ teaspoon ground ginger
½ teaspoon ground cinnamon
1 pound lamb, cut in cubes

2 tablespoons vegetable
  shortening
2 medium onions, thin sliced
1½ cups yogurt
1 teaspoon ground anise seeds
Salt to taste

Combine turmeric, coriander, crushed red peppers, garlic, ginger, and cinnamon. Mix well. Rub mixed spices into meat. Set aside for 1 hour. Heat vegetable shortening in large skillet. Fry onions until light brown. Add meat. Cook 4 or 5 minutes. Add yogurt. Stir well. Add anise and salt. Cook until meat is tender, approximately ½ hour. *Yield* 4 servings

LAMB AND POTATOES
[*Buckra Aloo*]

2 pounds lamb, cubed
2 tablespoons corn flour
2 tablespoons vegetable
  shortening
1 tablespoon crushed garlic
½ teaspoon ground ginger

¾ teaspoon ground cardamom
¼ teaspoon ground cloves
1 bay leaf, crushed
6 small potatoes, halved
Salt to taste

Heat dry skillet. Add meat. Singe meat quickly on all sides. Sprinkle corn flour over meat to coat. Add vegetable shortening. Fry 3 or 4 minutes. Add just enough water to loosen flour from pan. Mash together garlic and ginger. Add to meat. Mix well. Sprinkle cardamom, cloves, and bay leaf over meat. Add potatoes to skillet. Add water to half cover meat. Sprinkle on salt. Cover. Simmer until potatoes and meat are tender, approximately 1 hour. Serve. *Yield* 4 servings

LAMB AND VEGETABLE CURRY
[*Dhansak*]

4 cups lentils
2 pounds lamb, cubed
¼ cup chopped onion
2 medium potatoes, sliced
2 cups cubed pumpkin
2 small yams, cubed
¼ cup chopped parsley or coriander leaves
1 small squash, sliced
2 tablespoons mint
2 teaspoons chopped garlic

2 teaspoons ground marjoram
1 teaspoon ground cumin
¼ teaspoon ground fenugreek
¼ tablespoon ground oregano
1 tablespoon freshly ground black pepper
½ teaspoon cayenne
2 tablespoons vegetable shortening
1 large onion, sliced
½ tablespoon cumin seeds

Soak lentils in warm water for 1 hour in large pot. Cook slowly for 20 minutes or until half done. Add lamb, chopped onion, potatoes, pumpkin, yams, parsley, squash, mint, and garlic. Simmer until meat is tender, approximately 1 hour. Add marjoram, ground cumin, fenugreek, oregano, pepper, and cayenne. Mix well. Continue to simmer. Heat 2 tablespoons vegetable shortening in skillet. Add sliced onion and cumin seeds. Fry until onions are crisp. Add to meat along with shortening. Mix. Serve. *Yield* 6 to 8 servings

CURRY SOUP
[*Tanjore Palace*]

1¼ tablespoons freshly ground or crystallized ginger
1 tablespoon ground cumin
2 teaspoons salt
4 pounds loin lamb chops, fat trimmed
3 tablespoons vegetable shortening
2 large onions, finely sliced
1 teaspoon ground cinnamon
¼ teaspoon ground cloves
⅛ teaspoon ground mace
1 teaspoon ground turmeric
1 tablespoon ground coriander
½ teaspoon cayenne
1 teaspoon freshly ground black pepper
8 garlic cloves, crushed
1 tablespoon lentil or all-purpose flour
1 cup coconut milk
1 tablespoon ground cashew nuts
1 tablespoon ground poppy seeds
½ teaspoon ground cardamom
¼ teaspoon salt
Vegetable oil

Mix together ginger, cumin, and 2 teaspoons salt. Rub lamb chops with mixed spices. Heat vegetable shortening in Dutch oven or casserole. Add onions, cinnamon, cloves, mace, and turmeric. Fry 3 or 4 minutes. Add chops. Turn all chops so that they are coated with shortening and spices. Add water to cover 6 inches above chops. Cook slowly. Remove 1 cup of soup. Add coriander, cayenne, pepper, garlic, and lentil flour to cup of soup. Mix well. Return to cooking soup. Cook for 1 hour or until meat is tender. Skim fat off soup. Remove meat and reserve. Add coconut milk, cashew nuts, poppy seeds, cardamom, and ¼ teaspoon salt to soup. Stir soup. Simmer. Brush chops lightly with vegetable oil. Place high on broiler near flame. Broil on each side 2 or 3 minutes, or until chop is dry. Remove. Place 2 chops in each serving bowl. Pour hot soup over chops. Serve with wedges of lime, parsley, chutney, onion and carrot sambal, and boiled rice. *Yield* 8 to 10 servings

MEAT CURRY
[*Roghan Josh*]

1 *pound beef or lamb, cubed*
1 *cup yogurt*
1 *medium onion, quartered*
4 *slivers of garlic*
1 *four-inch piece of ginger*
½ *teaspoon paprika*
Whole dry red or green pepper
   to taste
¾ *teaspoon ground turmeric*
1 *tablespoon coriander seeds*
2 *tablespoons poppy seeds*
1 *tablespoon cumin seeds*

Chili powder to taste
6 *cloves*
1 *two-inch cinnamon stick*
1 *four-inch piece of coconut*
Salt to taste
1 *cup vegetable shortening*
1 *large onion, thinly sliced*
16 *almonds, blanched and*
   sliced
½ *teaspoon saffron*
¼ *cup milk*

Combine meat and yogurt in skillet. Cover and simmer until half cooked, approximately ½ hour. Place quartered onion, garlic, ginger, paprika, pepper, turmeric, coriander, poppy seeds, cumin, chili powder, cloves, cinnamon, coconut, and salt in food chopper using fine blade or in high-speed blender. Grind to a paste. Heat shortening in large skillet. Add sliced onion and quartered onion and spice paste. Fry until onions are browned for 15 minutes stirring all the time. Add meat and lightly fry until meat is browned. Add almonds. Simmer meat until tender, approximately ½ hour. Crush saffron in milk and add to meat. Cook 5 minutes more. *Yield* 4 to 5 servings

SPICED LAMB OR BEEF
[Vindaloo]

2 medium onions, quartered
3 slivers of garlic
1 one-inch piece of ginger
½ teaspoon ground turmeric
1 tablespoon cumin seeds
4 cloves
¼ teaspoon ground cinnamon

4 whole cardamoms
Salt to taste
2 tablespoons vegetable
   shortening
1 pound lamb or beef, cubed
½ cup vinegar

Place quartered onions, garlic, ginger, turmeric, cumin, cloves, cinnamon, cardamoms, and salt in food chopper using fine blade or in high-speed blender. Grind to a paste. Heat shortening in large skillet. Add ground spices and fry for 10 to 15 minutes continually stirring. Add meat and fry until brown. Add vinegar and cook on low heat until done, approximately ½ hour. If necessary add a little warm water. *Yield* 4 to 5 servings

SPICED POT ROAST
[Vindaloo Paste]

½ teaspoon crushed red
   pepper
16 garlic cloves
½ teaspoon ground cumin
1 teaspoon powdered mustard
¾ teaspoon ground turmeric
1¼ teaspoons ground ginger
1 tablespoon lemon pulp
1½ tablespoons sugar
1 teaspoon salt

3 tablespoons poppy seeds
½ cup vinegar
2 pounds beef, pork, or lamb,
   large cubes
4 tablespoons vegetable
   shortening
2 cloves
4 bay leaves
1 small onion, finely sliced
½ cup tomato purée

Place crushed red pepper, garlic, cumin, mustard, turmeric, ginger, lemon pulp, sugar, salt, poppy seeds, and vinegar in high-speed blender. Blend at high speed for 2 or 3 minutes. Place meat in large bowl. Pour blended spices over meat. Marinate for 2 hours. Heat vegetable shortening in Dutch oven or casserole. Add cloves and bay leaves. Fry 3 or 4 minutes. Add onions. Fry until onions are soft. Turn off heat. Allow oil to become lukewarm. Add meat. Simmer meat until half cooked. Add tomato purée. Increase heat and cook until meat is tender, approximately 1 hour. Strain off oil. Serve. *Yield* 10 to 12 servings
Note: Duck, small chickens, or shrimp may be substituted.

MEATBALLS
[*Shahi Kofta*]

1 *medium onion, quartered*	4 *tablespoons vegetable*
1 *one-inch piece of ginger*	*shortening*
6 *peppercorns*	1 *large onion, thinly sliced*
¼ *teaspoon ground cinnamon*	1 *tablespoon ground coriander*
¼ *teaspoon coriander seeds*	1 *teaspoon ground turmeric*
Whole dry green or red pep-	1 *tablespoon cumin seeds*
per, chopped to taste	*Chili powder to taste*
Pepper and salt to taste	*A few blades of mace*
1 *pound ground beef or*	¼ *teaspoon ground*
lamb	*cardamom*
1 *egg*	*Salt to taste*
	½ *cup water*

Place quartered onion, ginger, peppercorns, cinnamon, coriander, pepper and salt in food chopper. Use fine blades or high-speed blender. Grind to a paste. Place meat, egg, and ground onion with spices in mixing bowl. Mix well. Form into small meatballs. Heat shortening in large skillet and fry meatballs until light brown. Remove and keep warm. In same skillet, add sliced onion and brown. Add coriander, turmeric, cumin, chili powder, mace, cardamom, and salt. Fry for a few minutes. Add ½ cup water and meatballs. Cook until gravy is thick. *Yield* 4 to 5 servings

BEEF OR LAMB CURRY
[Pathani]

Vegetable oil for frying
4 pounds beef or lamb, cut in
  cubes
½ cup yogurt
2 teaspoons fennel seeds,
  ground
½ teaspoon ground ginger
1 teaspoon ground caraway
  seeds

1 teaspoon cayenne or red
  pepper
1 whole bay leaf
4 cloves, ground
2 teaspoons ground cinnamon
6 whole cardamoms, ground
2 teaspoons salt
½ teaspoon saffron, soaked
  in ¼ cup warm water

Place oil in large skillet and allow to become very hot. Add meat and turn each piece until brown all over. Add yogurt and continue cooking until yogurt dries up. Add all other ingredients except saffron. Sprinkle with very little hot water just in order to combine meat and spices. Cover. Cook until meat is done, approximately 1½ hours. Turn meat curry into serving dish and sprinkle with saffron water. Yield 12 to 14 servings

BEEF OR LAMB CURRY
[Olath]

2 tablespoon vegetable oil
2 teaspoons coriander seeds
½ teaspoon cayenne or red
  pepper
6 whole cardamoms
1 teaspoon ground turmeric

½ teaspoon salt
½ cup coconut bits, about
  ⅛"×½"
2 pounds lamb or beef, cut
  in cubes
½ cup sliced onions

Heat oil in small frying pan and add coriander, cayenne, cardamoms, turmeric, and salt. Fry for one minute until all the spices are well blended. Remove spices from pan and finely grind in food chopper or high-speed blender until very smooth. Rub meat with spices and set aside. Place coconut in a large skillet or Dutch oven and add just enough water to cover coconut and bring to a boil. Add meat to coconut and cook until meat is tender and water has evaporated, approximately 1 hour. Sauté onions in small amount of oil and add to meat. Turn meat in onions several times and remove to serving dish. *Yield* 4 to 6 servings

MEAT CURRY
[Butlers Korma]

2 *pounds chicken, beef, or lamb, cubed*	¼ *cup blanched almonds, sliced*
¼ *cup flour*	½ *teaspoon cayenne*
Salt to taste	½ *teaspoon mustard seeds*
4 *tablespoons vegetable shortening*	1 *teaspoon ground cumin*
2 *large onions, finely sliced*	2½ *teaspoons ground ginger*
⅛ *cup raisins*	4 *garlic cloves, crushed*
	1 *cup tomato purée*

Sprinkle meat with flour and salt. Set aside for ½ hour. Heat vegetable shortening in large skillet, or Dutch oven. Add onions. Fry until onions are soft. Remove half of onions and reserve. Fry remaining onions until crisp. Remove and drain. Add raisins and almonds to hot shortening. Fry 2 or 3 minutes. Remove and drain. Add cayenne, mustard seeds, cumin, ginger, and garlic. Fry 1 or 2 minutes. Add half cooked onions. Fry 2 or 3 minutes. Add meat. Brown on all sides. Cover. Simmer until meat is tender, approximately 1 hour. Add tomato purée. Cook until oil separates. Turn onto shallow dish. Garnish with crisp onions, raisins and almonds. *Yield* 4 to 6 servings

LEFTOVER MEAT
[*Jhal Fraezi*]

1 tablespoon vegetable
   shortening
1 small onion, finely sliced
¼ teaspoon fenugreek seed
1 teaspoon ground cumin

½ teaspoon ground turmeric
1 teaspoon cayenne
2 cups cold meat, diced
2 cups bouillon
Juice of ½ lime

Heat vegetable shortening in skillet. Add onion and fenugreek. Fry onion until light brown. Add cumin, turmeric, and cayenne. Fry 1 or 2 minutes. Add meat and bouillon. Simmer for 5 minutes or until gravy is thick. Sprinkle with lime juice. Serve. Yield 2 to 4 servings

TONGUE WITH LENTILS
[*Jeeb Masoor Dal*]

6 tablespoons vegetable
   shortening, divided
4 large onions, finely sliced,
   divided
1 cup lentils, soaked for 1 hour
4 small cooked lambs' tongues,
   sliced
Hot water

½ teaspoon chili powder
½ teaspoon ground turmeric
1 teaspoon ground coriander
1 teaspoon ground cumin
1¼ teaspoons ground ginger
6 garlic cloves, crushed
1 tablespoon salt
½ cup diced bell pepper

Heat 4 tablespoons vegetable shortening in large skillet. Add half of onions. Fry 2 or 3 minutes. Drain and add lentils. Fry until dry. Add sliced tongue. Add hot water to cover. Simmer until lentils are soft. Heat 2 tablespoons vegetable shortening in separate skillet. Add remaining half of onions. Fry 2 or 3 minutes. Add all spices and bell pepper. Fry 2 minutes. Pour over tongue. Mix. Cook until pepper is half cooked. Serve. Yield 8 to 10 servings

Fish and
Seafood Curries

SHRIMP AND SQUASH
[Lau Chingri]

2 tablespoons vegetable
  shortening
¼ teaspoon cumin seeds
1 bay leaf
Crushed red peppers to taste
½ teaspoon ground turmeric
½ teaspoon ground coriander

Chili powder to taste
1 pound squash, cubed and
  cooked
¼ pound cooked shrimp
Salt to taste
Sugar to taste
1 tablespoon milk

Heat vegetable shortening in skillet. Add cumin seeds, bay leaf, crushed red peppers, turmeric, coriander, and chili powder. Fry 2 minutes. Add squash, shrimp, salt, sugar, and milk. Simmer for 5 minutes. *Yield* 4 servings

BROILED INDIAN SHRIMP
[Malabari Jhinga]

1 pound raw shrimp
½ cup boiling water·
1 teaspoon salt
1 teaspoon ground coriander,
  divided
½ teaspoon instant minced
  onion
12 black peppercorns

¼ cup vegetable shortening
1½ teaspoons salt
½ teaspoon ground cumin
  seeds
1 teaspoon ground turmeric
2 teaspoons fresh lemon or
  lime juice
8 wedges fresh lemon or lime

Peel and devein raw shrimp. Set aside. Place in a saucepan with boiling water, the 1 teaspoon salt, ½ teaspoon of the coriander, instant minced onion, and black peppercorns. Bring to boiling point. Add peeled shrimp and cook 2 minutes or until shrimp begins to turn pink. Remove from heat and drain off water. Melt vegetable shortening. Add salt, remaining spices, and lemon or lime juice. Mix well. Stir in shrimp. Turn into a shallow pan. Spread over surface. Broil 5 minutes or until shrimp are pink and slightly browned around the edges. Serve with wedges of fresh lime or lemon. *Yield* 4 servings

SHRIMP BALLS
[*Jhinga Kofta*]

3 cups (3 cans, 5 ounces each) cooked, deveined shrimp
1 tablespoon instant minced onion
1 tablespoon water
2 eggs
1 teaspoon ground coriander
½ teaspoon ground cumin seeds
½ teaspoon powdered mustard
½ teaspoon ground tumeric
1 teaspoon salt*
⅛ teaspoon garlic powder
3 tablespoons flour
⅓ cup water
¼ cup evaporated milk or coconut milk
1 teaspoon fresh lemon juice
Vegetable shortening
Curry sauce

Put shrimp through a food chopper two times, using the finest blade. Soften instant minced onion in the 1 tablespoon water and add. Blend in eggs, spices, and flour. Mix until almost pastelike consistency. Add water and cook 5 minutes or until the mixture almost sticks to the pan. Shape into balls 1½ inches in diameter. Brown in melted shortening. Drain. Add to curry sauce. Cook gently 5 minutes. Add milk and heat 1 to 2 minutes. Do not stir, to prevent breaking shrimp balls. Add lemon juice and serve on rice. *Yield* 6 servings

* Eliminate salt if canned shrimp is used.

CURRY SAUCE
[*Masalah*]

¼ cup onion flakes
3 tablespoons water
2 tablespoons vegetable
  shortening

1¼ teaspoons curry powder
⅛ teaspoon garlic powder
¾ teaspoon salt
1¼ cups water

Soften onion flakes in the 3 tablespoons water. Fry in vegetable shortening until onions begin to brown. Add curry powder and garlic powder. Stir and cook 1 to 2 minutes. Add salt and water. Cook, uncovered, 10 minutes to form a medium-thick sauce. *Yield* 6 servings

FOR COCKTAIL SIZE: make ¾-inch balls and serve on toothpicks.

SHRIMP IN COCONUT SAUCE
[*Kadu Gurni*]

Crushed red peppers to taste
3 teaspoons ground mustard
1 teaspoon ground turmeric
2 cups shrimp, cleaned

½ coconut, grated
2 eggs
Salt to taste
½ cup vegetable shortening

Combine peppers, mustard, and turmeric in large bowl. Add shrimp and rub spices into shrimp. Reserve. Grind to a paste the coconut, 2 eggs, and salt. Use fine blade of food chopper or high-speed blender. Heat shortening in large skillet. Add shrimp. Fry slowly until done. Add coconut paste. Fry until paste is set. Serve hot. *Yield* 4 servings

SHRIMP AND POTATOES
[Chota Ginga Aloo Molee]

24 large shrimp, cleaned
1 teaspoon ground turmeric
Salt to taste
2 medium potatoes, cut in
   small cubes
4 garlic cloves
1¼ teaspoons ground ginger
½ teaspoon chili powder

¼ cup grated coconut
¼ teaspoon fenugreek seeds
¼ teaspoon oregano
4 tablespoons vegetable
   shortening
2 cups whole cocktail onions
½ cup thick coconut milk
2 tablespoons lime juice

Split shrimp down the back and open flat. Place shrimp, turmeric,
salt, and potatoes in large pan. Add water to cover. Boil until
shrimp are cooked. Place garlic, ginger, chili powder, coconut,
fenugreek, and oregano in food chopper. Use fine blade or high-
speed blender. Grind to a paste. Heat vegetable shortening in
large skillet. Add onions. Fry until soft. Add spice paste. Fry 2 or
3 minutes. Add cooked shrimp and potatoes. Add coconut milk.
Simmer until gravy starts to bubble. Add lime juice. Serve. *Yield*
4 servings

SHRIMP AND COCONUT
[Ginga Nariuz Kari]

2 cups shrimp, cleaned
½ cup chopped onions
4 tablespoons vegetable
   shortening
3 mint leaves, minced

½ cup grated coconut
1 small bell pepper
4 garlic cloves
1 teaspoon ground cumin
2 teaspoons lemon pulp

Heat dry large skillet. Add shrimp when skillet is hot. Turn shrimp
in dry skillet until they all curl. Lower heat. Add onions. Cover.
Heat vegetable shortening in another large skillet. Add mint. Fry
2 or 3 minutes. Grind to a paste: coconut, pepper, garlic, cumin,
and lemon pulp in food chopper. Use fine blade or high-speed

blender. Add to shortening. Fry 3 or 4 minutes. Add shrimp and onions. Mix well. Add hot water if gravy is too thick. Serve. *Yield* 4 servings

SHRIMP WITH TOMATO
[*Ginga Belatee Byngun*]

¼ *cup chick-pea or all-purpose flour*
½ *teaspoon salt*
¾ *teaspoon ground turmeric*
¼ *teaspoon cayenne*
½ *teaspoon celery salt*
2 *cups shrimp, cleaned, split down center*

4 *tablespoons vegetable shortening*
¼ *cup chopped chives*
½ *teaspoon ground ginger*
1 *teaspoon minced garlic*
½ *cup tomato paste*
½ *cup boiling water*

Combine chick-pea flour, salt, turmeric, cayenne, and celery salt. Roll shrimp in flour and coat well. Heat vegetable shortening in large skillet. Add chives, ginger, garlic, and tomato paste. Fry 2 or 3 minutes. Add shrimp. Mix well. Cover. Cook until shrimp turn pink. Add water to tomato-paste cup. Add to shrimp. Simmer for 10 minutes. *Yield* 4 servings

SHRIMP CURRY
[*Iral Eruvu*]

¼ *cup vegetable shortening*
1 *bay leaf*
3¼ *cups shrimp, divided*
1 *teaspoon crushed red peppers*
1 *garlic clove, crushed*

1¼ *teaspoons ground ginger*
1 *two-inch stick of cinnamon*
4 *cups coconut milk*
1 *tablespoon brown sugar*
¼ *cup unsweetened rhubarb*
Salt to taste

Heat vegetable shortening in large skillet. Add bay leaf. Fry 2 or 3 minutes. Place ¼ cup shrimp and crushed red pepper in wooden bowl and mash together. Add to skillet. Add remaining shrimp, garlic, ginger, and cinnamon. Fry for 3 or 4 minutes. Add coconut milk, brown sugar, rhubarb, and salt. Simmer until almost dry. *Yield* 4 servings

CURRIED SHELLFISH
[*Sothi*]

2 cups shrimp or crabmeat, cleaned
4 garlic cloves, crushed
¾ teaspoon ground ginger
¼ teaspoon chili powder
4 cups thick coconut milk

1 cup scallion tips, no green
½ teaspoon ground fenugreek
½ teaspoon ground mace
2 teaspoons ground poppy seeds

Place shrimp, garlic, ginger, chili powder, coconut milk, and scallions in casserole. Simmer slowly until scallions are tender. Add fenugreek, mace, and poppy seeds. Stir well. Simmer for 10 minutes. Serve. *Yield* 4 servings

SHRIMP CURRY
[*Jhinga Kari*]

2 pounds boiled shrimp, deveined
4 tablespoons grated coconut
2 tablespoons poppy seeds
1 teaspoon mustard seeds
¾ teaspoon turmeric
3 cloves garlic
1 large onion, quartered

¾ teaspoon ginger
2 teaspoons coriander
2 tablespoons tomato paste
Salt to taste
3 tablespoons vegetable shortening
1 cup water

Grind all the above in the blender, except the shrimp. Fry the mixture in 3 tablespoons shortening for 5 to 10 minutes, stirring constantly. Sprinkle water over mixture from time to time. Add shrimp and 1 cup water. Simmer 10 minutes. Serve with rice. *Yield* 4 servings

STEAMED FISH
[Machher Dam-Pokto]

1 *pound fish fillets, cod,*
flounder, halibut
1 *cup yogurt*
1¼ *teaspoons ground ginger*
Crushed red peppers to taste
2 *bay leaves*
2 *whole cardamoms*

2 *cloves*
1 *one-inch cinnamon stick*
8 *blanched almonds*
Salt to taste
Sugar to taste
1 *tablespoon butter or*
margarine

Mix all ingredients together. Place in steamer or pressure cooker. Cook until fish is done, approximately 15 minutes. Serve. *Yield* 4 servings

FISH-BALL CURRY
[Machher Ball Kari]

2 *cups cooked flaked fish*
½ *coconut, grated*
Crushed red peppers to taste
1 *small onion, whole*
1½ *teaspoons ground ginger,*
divided
1 *tablespoon tomato sauce*
1 *medium boiled potato*
1 *slice white bread, soaked in*
milk
7 *tablespoons vegetable*
shortening, divided
2 *medium potatoes, cubed*

1 *bay leaf*
2 *cloves*
1 *cardamom*
1 *one-inch cinnamon stick*
1 *large onion, finely sliced*
1 *small onion, minced*
½ *teaspoon ground turmeric*
½ *teaspoon ground cumin*
½ *teaspoon ground coriander*
¼ *teaspoon chili powder*
Sugar to taste
Salt to taste
2 *cups water*

Place fish, coconut, crushed red peppers, 1 small onion, ¾ teaspoon ginger, tomato sauce, boiled potato, bread, and salt in food chopper, or use high-speed blender. Grind. Form into small balls.

Heat 3 tablespoons vegetable shortening in large skillet. Fry fish balls until brown. Drain and reserve. In same skillet, add 1 tablespoon vegetable shortening. Add potato cubes. Fry until light brown. Drain and reserve. Heat 3 tablespoons vegetable shortening in casserole or Dutch oven. Add bay leaf, cloves, cardamom, and cinnamon. Fry 2 or 3 minutes. Add sliced onion. Fry until brown. Add minced onion, ¾ teaspoon ginger, turmeric, cumin, coriander, and chili powder. Add salt, sugar, potatoes, and water. Cook until potatoes are done. Add fish balls. Mix well. Remove. *Yield* 4 servings

FISH CURRY
[*Muchlee Paal Kari*]

4 *tablespoons vegetable*	½ *teaspoon ground turmeric*
shortening	½ *teaspoon cayenne*
6 *fillets, cod, halibut, flounder*	1 *teaspoon ground ginger*
1 *cup scallions, green removed*	1 *large onion*
2 *teaspoons ground coriander*	2 *cups thin coconut milk*

Heat vegetable shortening in large skillet. Fry fish a few fillets at a time. Set aside. Add scallions. Fry 2 or 3 minutes. Add fried fish. Grind together to a paste—coriander, turmeric, cayenne, ginger, and onion in food chopper. Use fine blade or high-speed blender. Pour coconut milk in bowl. Add spice paste. Mix well. Spread over fish. Cover skillet. Simmer for 5 minutes. Open. Turn fish over. Simmer 5 more minutes. Serve. *Yield* 6 servings

FISH AND COCONUT
[*Meen Partippu*]

1 *tablespoon vegetable*	½ *teaspoon cayenne*
shortening	½ *teaspoon ground turmeric*
½ *teaspoon mustard seeds*	1 *cup diced scallions*
2 *cups tuna fish, drained*	*Salt to taste*
½ *cup grated coconut, ground*	
to paste	

Heat vegetable shortening in skillet. Add mustard seeds. Fry until mustard seeds burst. Add all ingredients. Mix. Cover tightly. Cook over very low heat. Simmer for 1 hour. *Yield* 4 servings

CURRIED FISH
[*Muchlee Kari*]

¼ teaspoon minced garlic
¼ cup lemon juice
¾ teaspoon ground turmeric
½ teaspoon cayenne
1 tablespoon ground coriander
1 teaspoon ground cumin
¼ teaspoon ground fenugreek

¾ teaspoon ground ginger
4 tablespoons vegetable
  shortening
6 fillets, cod, halibut
½ cup chopped onion
2 teaspoons brown sugar

Soak garlic in lemon juice. Reserve. Combine turmeric, cayenne, coriander, cumin, fenugreek, and ginger. Rub spices into fillets. Heat vegetable shortening in skillet. Add fillets. Fry 2 or 3 minutes on each side. Add onions over fish. Cover. Cook until onions are soft. Add lemon juice with garlic and brown sugar. Simmer 10 minutes. Serve. *Yield* 4 to 6 servings

BAKED FISH IN LEAVES
[*Patreni Machchi*]

12 large romaine lettuce leaves
¼ cup parsley
⅛ cup mint leaves
½ teaspoon black pepper
1 tablespoon lemon pulp
1 teaspoon fenugreek
2 teaspoons curry powder

2 teaspoons salt
2 tablespoons brown sugar
Vinegar to make paste
12 soles, flounders, or any
  flatfish fillets
6 teaspoons butter, divided

Wash and dry romaine leaves. Place all remaining ingredients except fish, vinegar, and butter in food chopper. Use fine blade or high-speed blender. Grind to a paste. Beat in sufficient vinegar to make paste-spreading consistency. Sandwich each pair of fillets with some of the spice mixture. Wrap the "sandwich" in romaine to completely cover. Place in Pyrex casserole. Top each piece with 1 teaspoon butter. Bake in hot oven until leaves are baked brown and wilted. About 40 minutes. Serve hot, with leaves intact. *Yield* 6 servings

POTATO AND FISH CURRY
[*Machher Charchari*]

2 tablespoons vegetable shortening

1 pound cod or halibut steaks, cubed

1¼ teaspoons ground turmeric, divided

Salt to taste

2 large potatoes, cut in ¼-inch slices

2 medium onions, finely sliced

¼ teaspoon chili powder

½ teaspoon crushed red peppers

Heat vegetable shortening in skillet. Dust fish with 1 teaspoon turmeric and salt. Place fish in skillet. Fry until brown. Drain and reserve. Add potatoes to skillet. Fry 3 or 4 minutes. Drain and reserve. Add onions to skillet. Brown onions. Add ¼ teaspoon turmeric, chili powder, and salt. Fry 2 minutes. Return potatoes to skillet. Add enough water to cover. Add crushed red peppers. Cook potatoes until half done. Add fish. Cover. Cook until potatoes and fish are cooked and gravy is thick. *Yield* 4 servings

COCONUT MILK AND FISH
[*Machher Mauli*]

3 tablespoons vegetable shortening

2 large onions, finely sliced

½ teaspoon crushed red peppers

1 cup thick coconut milk

1 pound fish steaks, cod or halibut

Salt to taste

Juice of 1 lemon

Heat vegetable shortening in skillet. Add onions and crushed red peppers. Fry until golden brown. Add 4 tablespoons coconut milk. Cook 1 minute. Add fish and remaining coconut milk. Add salt. Cover. Simmer until fish is cooked. Add lemon juice. *Yield* 4 servings

PICKLED FISH
[*Muchlee Padda*]

½ *tablespoon ground turmeric*
1 *tablespoon salt*
½ *tablespoon paprika*
1 *cup vegetable oil*
2 *pounds cod or halibut, cut in large cubes*

1 *cup raisins*
1 *tablespoon ground cumin*
1 *tablespoon ground mustard*
1 *tablespoon ground ginger*
1 *tablespoon crushed garlic*
2 *tablespoons lemon pulp*
4 *cups vinegar*

Combine turmeric, salt, and paprika. Dust fish with combined spices. Heat vegetable oil in large skillet. Fry fish a few pieces at a time until brown on all sides. Remove fish to large platter. Reserve oil. Place raisins, cumin, mustard, ginger, garlic, and lemon pulp in food chopper. Use fine blade or high-speed blender, adding just enough vinegar for grinding to smooth and creamy paste. Dilute raisin paste in remaining vinegar. Pour over fish. Coat all fish pieces equally. Pack fish into large jar or crock. Pour all vinegar, spices, and oil remaining from skillet into jar or crock. Cover tightly. Pickle for 2 days. *Yield* 6 to 8 servings

FISH AND COCONUT MILK
[*Muchlee Nariul*]

1 teaspoon salt
¼ teaspoon cayenne
½ teaspoon ground black
  pepper
¼ teaspoon ground cumin
½ teaspoon ground turmeric
6 fillets, cod, halibut, flounder

3 tablespoons vegetable
  shortening
1 large onion, finely sliced
1¼ teaspoons ground ginger
6 garlic cloves, crushed
½ cup tomato purée
2 cups coconut milk
Juice of 1 lime

Combine salt, cayenne, pepper, cumin, and turmeric. Sprinkle fish with spices. Set aside. Heat vegetable shortening in large skillet. Add onion. Fry until crisp. Add ginger and garlic. Fry 2 or 3 minutes. Add tomato purée. Heat to boiling, stirring all the time. Add coconut milk. Wait until it boils. Lower heat. Add fish. Sprinkle lime juice over fish. Simmer for 10 minutes. *Yield* 6 servings

Vegetable and Egg Curries

OKRA CURRY
[Bhindi Kari]

4 tablespoons vegetable
 shortening, divided
36 three-inch pieces of okra
¾ cup chopped onion,
 divided
1 teaspoon crushed garlic
2 teaspoons ground ginger
1 tablespoon ground coriander

½ teaspoon cayenne
½ teaspoon ground turmeric
¼ cup unsweetened cooked
 rhubarb
¼ cup molasses
1 teaspoon mustard seeds
1 teaspoon lentil flour

Heat 3 tablespoons vegetable shortening in skillet. Place okra in skillet. Fry until browned all over. Reduce heat. Add ¼ cup onion, garlic, and ginger. Stir slowly until all juices have been absorbed. Sprinkle on coriander, cayenne, and turmeric. Add rhubarb and molasses. Stir in. Simmer until gravy is reduced. Heat 1 tablespoon vegetable shortening in small skillet. Add mustard seeds. Fry until they stop sputtering. Add lentil flour. Stir. Add ½ cup chopped onion. Fry until onions are brown. Pour into skillet with okra. Remove some gravy from okra skillet. Add to small skillet. Heat. Return gravy to large skillet. Serve. *Yield 6 servings*

CABBAGE FOOGATH

1 cup water
½ teaspoon cumin seeds
½ teaspoon turmeric
2 teaspoons salt
2 cups shredded cabbage
¼ cup grated coconut
2 tablespoons vegetable
  shortening

½ small onion, finely chopped
2 small garlic cloves, finely
  chopped
¼ teaspoon fenugreek
¼ teaspoon mustard seeds
2 teaspoons split peas, soaked
  for 1 hour

Boil water in large pan. Add cumin seeds, turmeric, and salt. Boil
for 4 to 5 minutes. Add cabbage and cover. Boil for 4 to 5 minutes.
Strain cabbage. Add coconut. Cover and keep warm. Heat vegetable shortening in small skillet. Add onion. Fry until crisp. Add
garlic, fenugreek, mustard seeds, and split peas. Fry until seeds
stop bursting. Add to cabbage. Serve. *Yield* 2 servings

VEGETABLES AND SPICES
[*Vendai Kai Masalah*]

2 cups unsweetened rhubarb
½ teaspoon crushed red
  peppers
8 crushed garlic cloves,
  divided
2 tablespoons vegetable
  shortening
½ pound okra, cut ends

3 medium onions, finely
  sliced
2½ teaspoons ground ginger
1 teaspoon ground turmeric
1 tablespoon ground coriander
3 tablespoons finely ground
  coconut
1 teaspoon mustard seeds

Pour rhubarb in small bowl; add peppers, 4 crushed garlic cloves.
Reserve. Heat shortening in large skillet. Fry okra until soft. Remove okra and set aside. Add onions to same skillet and fry light
brown. Add ginger, remaining garlic, and fry for 5 minutes. Add
turmeric and coriander and fry 2 or 3 minutes. Add reserved

rhubarb juice and bring to a boil. Add okra and let simmer for a
few minutes. Add coconut. Fry mustard seeds in a large spoon with
a bit of shortening. When seeds burst, add to okra. *Yield* 4
servings

OKRA AND COCONUT
[*Dahi Bhinda*]

1 tablespoon vegetable shortening	½ teaspoon ground ginger
	1½ cups yogurt
¼ pound okra, cut in halves	Chili powder
Salt to taste	½ teaspoon ground coriander
½ teaspoon ground turmeric	¼ coconut, grated

Heat vegetable shortening in large skillet. Add okra. Fry for 5
minutes. Add salt, turmeric, and ginger. Fry until okra is done.
Combine yogurt, chili powder, coriander, and coconut. Mix
well. Add to okra and serve. *Yield* 4 servings

TOMATOES AND EGGPLANT
[*Ambal*]

3 tablespoons vegetable shortening	2 teaspoons vinegar
	1 teaspoon salt
1 cups cubed eggplant, ½-inch size	4 cups cubed tomatoes, ½-inch size
1 teaspoon mustard seeds	2 teaspoons raisins
½ teaspoon cayenne	

Heat vegetable shortening in skillet. Add eggplant. Fry until
brown all over. Remove and drain. Add mustard seeds to skillet.
Fry until they stop sputtering. Add cayenne. Add vinegar and salt.
Add fried eggplant. Cover. Cook for 4 or 5 minutes. Add tomatoes
and raisins. Mix. Cook until raisins are plump. *Yield* 4 to 6
servings

EGGPLANT
[*Bhaja-Maslar Tarkari*]

2 *tablespoons vegetable
  shortening*
¼ *teaspoon fenugreek seeds*
¼ *teaspoon crushed red
  peppers*
6 *slices eggplant, ½ inch thick*
½ *cup yogurt*

½ *cup water*
½ *teaspoon salt*
1 *tablespoon sugar*
¼ *teaspoon chili powder*
¾ *teaspoon ground mustard*
¾ *teaspoon ground cumin*

Heat vegetable shortening in skillet. Add fenugreek seeds and
crushed red peppers. Fry 2 or 3 minutes. Add eggplant. Fry 3 or 4
minutes. Combine yogurt, water, salt, sugar, and chili powder.
Add to skillet. Cover. Cook until eggplant is tender. Add mustard
and cumin. Mix well. Remove from heat. *Yield* 4 servings

EGGPLANT, ONION, AND TOMATO
[*Bhurta*]

2 *medium eggplants*
1 *medium onion, finely
  chopped*
2 *tablespoons vegetable
  shortening*

2 *medium tomatoes, chopped*
½ *teaspoon ground cumin*
1 *teaspoon ground coriander*
½ *cup yogurt*
Salt and pepper to taste

Cook eggplants unpeeled in medium oven for 45 minutes or until
eggplant is very soft to touch. Sauté onion in vegetable shortening
until light brown. Add tomatoes, cumin, coriander, and cook until
soft. Peel skin off eggplant and chop fine. Add eggplant and
yogurt to onion-and-tomato mixture, also salt and pepper to taste.
Mix well and cook 15 to 20 minutes stirring occasionally until
water is absorbed. *Yield* 4 servings

FRIED EGGPLANT
[*Wangyachen Bharit*]

3 tablespoons vegetable
shortening
3 medium onions, finely
sliced
1 garlic clove, crushed

¼ teaspoon ground cumin
¼ teaspoon ground turmeric
Chili powder to taste
Salt to taste
1 pound eggplant, sliced

Heat vegetable shortening in large skillet. Add onions; fry until brown. Add garlic, cumin, turmeric, chili powder, and salt. Add eggplant. Fry until tender. *Yield* 4 servings

EGGPLANT AND COCONUT
[*Pinju Katharikai Vadhakkal*]

1 tablespoon lentil flour
¼ coconut, grated
1 tablespoon ground coriander
Crushed red pepper to taste
¼ cup vegetable shortening
2 medium eggplants

¾ teaspoon ground cloves
½ teaspoon ground nutmeg
½ teaspoon ground mace
Salt to taste
½ cup rhubarb

Grind together to a paste: lentil flour, coconut, coriander, and crushed red pepper in food grinder using fine blade or high-speed blender. Heat vegetable shortening in casserole or Dutch oven. Fry coconut paste for 3 or 4 minutes. Slit eggplant lengthwise into four pieces, but do not completely cut. Rub fried coconut spices into eggplant slits. Reheat vegetable shortening and fry cloves, nutmeg, mace, and salt. Fry for 2 or 3 minutes. Add eggplant and pour rhubarb over eggplant. Simmer until eggplants are tender. *Yield* 4 servings

SPICED EGGPLANT
[*Katharikai Rasavangi*]

2 tablespoons vegetable
   shortening, divided
½ teaspoon split peas
1 teaspoon lentils
2 teaspoons ground coriander
   seeds
Crushed red pepper to taste
¼ coconut, grated

2 medium-size eggplants,
   1-inch slices
1 cup unsweetened rhubarb
1 cup water
1 teaspoon ground turmeric
Salt to taste
2 teaspoons mustard seeds

Heat 1 tablespoon vegetable shortening in skillet. Add split peas, lentils, coriander, crushed red pepper, and coconut. Fry for 3 or 4 minutes. Remove from skillet into food chopper and grind to paste using fine blade or high-speed blender. Place eggplant in pot. Add rhubarb, water, turmeric, and salt. Cook for ½ hour. Add paste and mix well. Heat 1 tablespoon vegetable shortening in large spoon. Add mustard seeds. Fry for 2 or 3 minutes. Add to eggplant. *Yield* 4 servings

PEA CURRY
[*Pattani Moli*]

2 teaspoons vegetable
   shortening
6 small white onions
¾ teaspoon ground ginger
1 garlic clove, crushed
½ teaspoon ground cinnamon
½ teaspoon ground mace
¼ teaspoon ground
   cardamom

½ teaspoon ground turmeric
¼ cup tomato purée
¼ teaspoon ground cloves
1 teaspoon rice flour
2 cups thick coconut milk or
   buttermilk
2 cups half-cooked peas
Crushed red pepper to taste
1 cup cashew nuts, fried

Heat vegetable shortening in skillet. Add onions, ginger, garlic, cinnamon, mace, cardamom, turmeric, tomato purée, cloves, and rice flour, stirring as each ingredient is added. Do not allow onions to brown. Add coconut milk, peas, crushed red pepper, and nuts. Simmer until peas are tender. Serve with rice. *Yield* 4 servings

FRIED PEPPERS
[*Mothya Mirachyanchi Bhaj*]

2 tablespoons vegetable shortening
½ teaspoon mustard seeds
6 medium green bell peppers, finely chopped
¼ cup lentil flour
¼ coconut, grated
½ teaspoon ground coriander
Salt to taste

Heat vegetable shortening in large skillet. Add mustard seeds. Fry until they burst. Add chopped green peppers. Simmer until peppers are tender. Add lentil flour, coconut, coriander, and salt. Mix well. Fry for 5 minutes. *Yield* 4 servings

GREEN PEPPER CURRY
[*Pulippu Kari*]

8 green bell peppers, stems and seeds removed
1 cup diced rhubarb
2 tablespoons vegetable shortening
2 medium onions, sliced thin, divided
¼ teaspoon curry powder
¾ teaspoon ground mustard
½ teaspoon ground ginger
½ garlic clove, crushed
Salt to taste
Brown sugar to taste

Boil peppers in water to cover until three quarters done. Drain and reserve just enough water to cook rhubarb in. Cook rhubarb in pepper water. Pour rhubarb into strainer, reserving rhubarb juice. Press rhubarb pulp so all juice is out; reserve. Heat vegetable shortening in large skillet or casserole. Fry half of onions until crisp. Drain and set aside. Add curry, mustard, remaining onion, ginger, and garlic. Fry for 2 or 3 minutes. Add rhubarb juice and peppers. Cook until peppers are done. Add salt and brown sugar. Bring to a boil. Remove and garnish with crisp onions. Serve with yogurt and rice. *Yield* 4 servings

Note: If to be served with roast lamb, reduce amount of sugar.

POTATO PATTIES
[*Aloo Vadai*]

2 cups hot mashed potatoes
2 tablespoons chopped onions
2 tablespoons ground ginger
¼ cup chopped cashew nuts
¼ cup chopped parsley
2 tablespoons chopped
  pimento

2 tablespoons chopped bell
  pepper
¼ cup tomato purée
1 teaspoon salt
2 tablespoons chick-pea flour
2 tablespoons rice flour
Vegetable oil for frying

Combine all ingredients. Blend well. Form into thin patties. Heat vegetable shortening in skillet. Fry. Drain before serving. *Yield* 4 to 6 servings

POTATOES WITH GRAVY
[*Bata Ne Tameta*]

2 tablespoons vegetable
  shortening
½ teaspoon mustard seeds
2 medium potatoes, peeled
  and diced
1 medium tomato, sliced
½ teaspoon ground coriander

Crushed red peppers to taste
½ teaspoon ground ginger
½ teaspoon ground turmeric
Chili powder to taste
½ teaspoon sugar
Salt to taste

Heat vegetable shortening in large skillet. Add mustard seeds and fry until they burst. Add potatoes. Fry 2 or 3 minutes. Add water to half cover potatoes. Cook until almost done. Add tomato and remaining ingredients. Simmer until tomato becomes pulpy. *Yield* 4 servings

POTATO CURRY
[*Gol Amleenu Shak*]

2 tablespoons vegetable
  shortening
1 teaspoon mustard seeds
Crushed red peppers to taste
2 large boiled potatoes, diced
2 teaspoons chick-pea flour

1 cup unsweetened cooked
  rhubarb
1 teaspoon ground turmeric
2 teaspoons ground coriander
1 teaspoon ground cumin
2 teaspoons brown sugar
Salt to taste

Heat vegetable shortening in large skillet. Add mustard seeds and crushed red peppers. Fry until mustard seeds burst. Add potatoes. Fry 2 or 3 minutes, then stir in remaining ingredients. Bring to a boil. Remove from heat. *Yield* 4 servings

SPICED POTATOES IN YOGURT
[*Aloo Ka Bharta*]

2 tablespoons water
⅛ teaspoon coriander
⅛ teaspoon mint leaves
Whole dry green or red
  pepper, chopped, to taste
¼ teaspoon ground pepper
¼ teaspoon ground cinnamon
¼ teaspoon ground
  cardamom

Salt to taste
1 tablespoon vegetable
  shortening
1 tablespoon lemon juice
6 medium white potatoes,
  boiled, peeled, and diced
½ cup yogurt

Blend together all the spices in water. Heat vegetable shortening in large skillet. Add spices, lemon juice, and potatoes. Fry until all are mixed well. Remove skillet from heat and blend in yogurt. *Yield* 4 to 6 servings

MASHED POTATOES
[Urulai Kizhangu Podimas]

1 tablespoon vegetable   ½ teaspoon ground turmeric
  shortening   2 cups hot mashed potatoes
2 teaspoons split peas, soaked   Salt to taste
½ teaspoon mustard seeds   ¼ coconut, grated
Crushed red pepper to taste   Juice of 1 lime
½ teaspoon ground ginger

Heat vegetable shortening in large skillet. Add split peas and
mustard seeds. Fry until mustard seeds burst. Add crushed red
pepper, ginger, and turmeric. Add potatoes and salt. Remove from
heat. Add coconut and lime juice. Mix and serve. *Yield* 4 servings

STRING BEANS AND POTATOES
[Papdeenu Undhiyun]

3 tablespoons vegetable   1 small eggplant, peeled and
  shortening   cubed
½ pound string beans, string   2 small boiled sweet potatoes,
  and cut in half   peeled and cubed
3 teaspoons ground ginger   2 small boiled white potatoes,
Crushed red peppers to taste   peeled and cubed
½ teaspoon ground coriander   2 bananas, sliced
Salt to taste   1 coconut, grated

Heat vegetable shortening in large skillet. Add string beans, ginger,
crushed red peppers, coriander, and salt. Fry for 10 minutes. Add
eggplant, potatoes, and bananas. Fry for 5 minutes. Add coconut
and cook slowly until all vegetables are tender. *Yield* 4 servings

POTATOES
[Heenger Aloor—Dam]

2 tablespoons vegetable
  shortening
1 pound small potatoes,
  boiled and peeled
Crushed red peppers to taste
3 cloves
½ teaspoon ground cinnamon

¼ teaspoon ground
  cardamom
¾ teaspoon ground ginger
½ cup yogurt, divided
4 tablespoons water,
  divided
Salt to taste
1 teaspoon sugar

Heat vegetable shortening in skillet. Add potatoes. Fry until light brown. Remove and drain on paper. In same skillet, add crushed red peppers, cloves, cinnamon, and cardamom. Fry 2 or 3 minutes, mixing while frying. Add ginger, 1 tablespoon yogurt, and 1 tablespoon water. Fry 3 or 4 minutes. Combine 3 tablespoons of water, salt, sugar, and remaining yogurt. Add to skillet. Add drained potatoes. Mix well. Cover tightly. Simmer for 5 minutes. *Yield* 4 servings

CAULIFLOWER CURRY
[Doi Phul Cobi]

3 large onions, finely sliced,
  divided
½ garlic clove
¾ teaspoon ground ginger
Salt to taste
½ teaspoon turmeric
1 cup yogurt

1 pound cauliflower buds
2 tablespoons vegetable
  shortening
2 cloves
1 two-inch cinnamon stick
2 cardamoms

Place ½ of the onions with garlic and ginger in food chopper. Use fine blade or high-speed blender. Grind together to a paste. Divide in 2 equal portions. Add ½ of ginger paste, turmeric, and

salt to yogurt. Mix well. Coat the yogurt onto the cauliflower
buds; stuff the mixture well into the crevices. Heat vegetable
shortening in skillet. Add remaining onions. Fry until light brown.
Add cloves, cinnamon, cardamoms, and remaining ginger paste.
Fry for 5 minutes. Add cauliflower. Fry slowly. Sprinkle with a
little water. Cover. Simmer until cauliflower is done. Add vegetable shortening at short intervals to prevent sticking. *Yield* 4
servings

FRESH CAULIFLOWER AND PEAS
[*Gobi Matar Ki Tarkari*]

3 *tablespoons vegetable*
  shortening
¾ *teaspoon ground cumin*
  seeds
¼ *teaspoon ground black*
  pepper
4 *teaspoons ground coriander*
1 *teaspoon ground turmeric*

3 *tablespoons water*
1 *large head cauliflower*
  (*about 2½ pounds*)
½ *cup chopped onion* (1
  medium onion)
1 *cup shelled fresh peas*
1 *bay leaf*
2¼ *teaspoons salt*

Heat vegetaĥle shortening in Dutch oven or casserole. Blend
cumin, black pepper, coriander, and turmeric with 3 tablespoons
water. Stir in hot vegetable shortening, cook over low heat for
2 minutes, or until spices have been cooked, stirring constantly.
Add cauliflower broken into small flowerets, onion, peas, bay leaf,
and salt. Mix thoroughly. Cover tightly and cook 10 to 15 minutes
on medium heat or until just tender. *Yield* 8 to 10 servings

SPINACH
[*Palak Ka Sag*]

2 *large bunches of spinach*
2 *tablespoons vegetable*
  shortening
2 *large onions, finely chopped*

Whole dry red or green
  pepper, chopped, to taste
Salt to taste

Wash and cut spinach. Heat vegetable shortening in skillet and fry onions until brown; add chopped pepper. Add spinach. Cover and cook over low heat until dry. Add salt and stir. *Yield* 4 servings

KIDNEY BEANS
[*Valni Dal*]

½ cup kidney beans, soak overnight, drain
1 tablespoon vegetable shortening
½ teaspoon mustard seeds

Chili powder to taste
Salt to taste
½ teaspoon ground turmeric
½ tablespoon butter or margarine

Heat vegetable shortening in skillet. Add mustard seeds and chili powder. Fry until mustard seeds burst. Add beans, salt, and turmeric. Fry 3 or 4 minutes. Add water to cover. Simmer until beans are done. Before serving, add ½ tablespoon of melted butter or margarine. *Yield* 4 servings

LENTILS AND VEGETABLES
[*Kootu*]

1 cup cooked lentils
1 large yam or sweet potato, cubed and peeled
½ medium summer squash, cubed
½ teaspoon ground turmeric
¼ teaspoon chili powder

Salt to taste
¼ coconut, ground
1 tablespoon vegetable shortening
¼ coconut, grated
1 teaspoon mustard seeds

Place lentils, yam, squash, turmeric, and chili powder in pan with just enough water to cover. Cook until vegetables are tender. Add salt and cook for 5 minutes more. Add ground coconut. Mix well. Bring to a boil and remove from fire. Heat vegetable shortening in skillet. Fry grated coconut and mustard seeds, for 3 or 4 minutes. Add to vegetables and mix well. *Yield* 4 servings

PUMPKIN CURRY
[*Erisheri*]

½ *coconut, grated*
3 *teaspoons ground mustard*
½ *cup yogurt*
1 *teaspoon vegetable*
  shortening

¼ *teaspoon curry powder*
2 *teaspoons lentils, soaked*
2 *cups small cubes of cooked*
  pumpkin

Grind coconut and mustard to a smooth paste in food chopper using fine blade or high-speed blender. Add to yogurt. Heat vegetable shortening in large round spoon. Add curry and lentils. Fry until lentils are crisp. Place pumpkin in serving bowl. Mix in yogurt and coconut paste. Mix in fried curry and lentils with same spoon. *Yield* 4 servings

PUMPKIN OR SQUASH
[*Lal Bhopalyachi Bhaji*]

2 *tablespoons vegetable*
  shortening
¼ *teaspoon mustard seeds*
¼ *teaspoon ground turmeric*
¼ *teaspoon ground coriander*
2 *small bay leaves*
1 *small onion, finely chopped*
½ *teaspoon ground ginger*
1 *garlic clove, crushed*

Crushed red peppers to taste
½ *pound pumpkin or squash,*
  peeled and cut in 1-inch
  cubes
2 *medium tomatoes, sliced*
Salt to taste
⅔ *cup yogurt*
¼ *coconut, grated*

Heat shortening in large skillet. Add mustard seeds, turmeric, coriander, bay leaves, onion, ginger, garlic, and crushed red peppers. Fry for 5 minutes. Add pumpkin, tomatoes, and salt. Simmer until pumpkin is tender. Add yogurt. Garnish with coconut and serve. *Yield* 4 servings

ZUCCHINI CURRY
[*Kai Puli Pachadi*]

2 *pounds zucchini, cut in*
pieces
1 *teaspoon ground turmeric*
Crushed red peppers to taste
6 *teaspoons ground mustard*

2 *tablespoons sesame seeds*
2 *tablespoons grated coconut*
1 *teaspoon vegetable*
shortening
1 *cup unsweetened rhubarb*

Place zucchini in water to cover. Cook until tender. Drain. Grind together to a paste turmeric, crushed red peppers, mustard, sesame, and coconut, in food chopper using fine blade or high-speed blender. Heat vegetable shortening in large skillet. Add ground spiced coconut paste. Fry for 2 or 3 minutes. Add rhubarb a little at a time until all is in the skillet. Mix well. Bring to a boil. Add zucchini. Remove from heat. *Yield* 4 servings

SQUASH AND BEANS
[*Olan*]

3 *cups cubed squash, ½-inch*
cubes
2 *cups lima beans*
2 *cups thick coconut milk*
1¼ *teaspoons ground cumin*

1 *teaspoon peppercorns,*
ground
Crushed red peppers to taste
Salt to taste

Cook squash and beans in sufficient water to cover. Simmer until cooked. Add coconut milk, cumin, ground peppercorns, crushed red peppers, and salt. Mix. Bring to a boil. *Yield* 4 servings

FRUIT AND RICE CURRY
[*Mangai Chithranam*]

1 tablespoon mustard seeds	1 teaspoon ground turmeric
Crushed red peppers to taste	1 tablespoon lentils, soaked
½ coconut, grated	⅛ teaspoon curry powder
Salt to taste	2 cups cooked rice
¼ cup vegetable shortening	2 cups diced ripe cantaloupe

Grind together to a paste, mustard seeds, crushed red peppers, coconut, and salt. Use food chopper with fine blade or high-speed blender. Heat vegetable shortening in large skillet. Fry turmeric, lentils, and curry. Place rice in serving bowl. Add cantaloupe, coconut paste, and fried spices. Mix well. *Yield* 4 servings

COUNTRY CAPTAIN VEGETABLES

¼ cup chopped onion	1 cup diced cold cooked
2 garlic cloves, minced	carrots
1 tablespoon vegetable	1 cup cold cooked peas
shortening	1 cup diced cold cooked
1 tablespoon water	potatoes
2 teaspoons curry powder	2 teaspoons cider vinegar
	1½ teaspoons salt

Sauté onion and garlic in shortening along with curry powder 2 to 3 minutes. Add water, vegetables, vinegar, and salt. Cook only until hot. Serve with grated fresh coconut or dried coconut sprinkled over the top. *Yield* 6 servings

VEGETABLES AND YOGURT
[*Kalan*]

1½ medium yams or sweet
  potatoes, cubed
2 zucchini, cut in 1-inch pieces
1 teaspoon black pepper
1 teaspoon ground turmeric
Salt to taste

4 cups yogurt
½ cup coconut, ground to
  paste
1 tablespoon vegetable
  shortening
2 teaspoons mustard

Place yams and zucchini in pan with water to cover. Add pepper
and turmeric. Cook until vegetables are tender. Add salt. Cook
vegetables until water has boiled out. Add yogurt and cook until
half of yogurt has cooked away. Remove from heat. Add coconut
paste and mix well. Heat vegetable shortening in large round
spoon. Add mustard seeds and fry until they burst. Add to
vegetables with same spoon. *Yield* 4 servings

CHEESE AND VEGETABLE CURRY
[*Chhanar Dalna*]

3 tablespoons vegetable
  shortening
¼ pound unsalted farmer
  cheese, cut in cubes
2 cloves
2 teaspoons ground cinnamon
⅛ teaspoon ground cardamom
⅛ teaspoon crushed red
  peppers
1¼ teaspoons ground ginger

1 teaspoon ground turmeric
¼ teaspoon chili powder
½ teaspoon ground cumin
1 large tomato, cubed
3 medium potatoes, diced
Salt to taste
Sugar to taste
1 cup water
Juice of 1 lemon

Heat vegetable shortening in large skillet. Add cheese. Fry 2 or 3
minutes. Be careful when turning not to break cheese. Remove
cheese and reserve. In same skillet add cloves, cinnamon, carda-

mom, and crushed red peppers. Fry 1 minute. Add ginger, turmeric, chili powder, and cumin. Fry for 5 minutes. Add tomato, potatoes, salt, sugar, and water. Cook until potatoes are done. Add cheese. Gently mix. Sprinkle with lemon. Serve. *Yield* 4 servings

MADRAS EGG CURRY
[*Moote Kari*]

¼ *cup chopped onion*	1 *tablespoon tomato paste*
4 *garlic cloves, minced*	¾ *cup water*
1 *tablespoon vegetable*	1 *teaspoon salt*
shortening	1 *teaspoon fresh lemon juice*
2 *teaspoons curry powder*	6 *hard-cooked eggs*

Sauté onion and garlic in shortening along with curry powder 3 to 4 minutes. Add tomato paste and water. Cook 3 to 4 minutes. Add salt and lemon juice. Stir and cook until the gravy is of medium thickness, about 1 minute. Peel hard-cooked eggs cut in half lengthwise and add. Heat. Serve with rice. *Yield* 5 servings

EGGS AND CAULIFLOWER
[*Andeghaloon Cauliflower Bhaji*]

3 *tablespoons vegetable*	*Crushed red peppers to taste*
shortening	*Salt to taste*
1 *large onion, finely sliced*	½ *teaspoon ground coriander*
½ *teaspoon ground turmeric*	1½ *cups cooked cauliflower,*
1 *garlic clove, crushed*	*chopped*
½ *teaspoon ground ginger*	2 *eggs*

Heat vegetable shortening in skillet. Add onion. Fry until brown. Add turmeric, garlic, ginger, crushed red peppers, salt, and coriander. Add cauliflower. Mix well. Fry for 4 or 5 minutes. Add eggs. Mix. Fry until eggs are cooked. *Yield* 4 servings

SPICED EGGS
[*Masalyachi Andi*]

¼ coconut, grated
Chili powder to taste
⅛ teaspoon ground black
    pepper
⅛ teaspoon ground cloves
½ teaspoon ground cinnamon

Salt to taste
4 hard-boiled eggs
1 tablespoon vegetable
    shortening
1 medium onion, finely sliced

Place coconut, chili powder, pepper, cloves, cinnamon, and salt in food chopper. Use fine blade or high-speed blender. Grind to a paste. Make a slit lengthwise in eggs; be careful not to split them. Fill ½ of paste in slit of eggs. Tie eggs with string or thread. Heat vegetable shortening in skillet. Add onion. Fry until brown. Add eggs and enough water to cover. Bring to a boil. Remove from heat. *Yield* 4 servings

Curried Kebabs, Chops, and Cutlets

LAMB CHOPS
[Moghlai Chop]

½ teaspoon ground ginger
8 garlic cloves, crushed
¾ teaspoon ground turmeric
Chili powder to taste
Salt to taste
2 tablespoons vinegar
8 lamb chops, bone and
   fat removed

6 tablespoons vegetable
   shortening, divided
2 medium boiled potatoes,
   peeled and sliced
2 medium onions, thinly
   sliced

Combine ginger, garlic, turmeric, chili powder, salt, and vinegar. Mix well. Rub on chops and set aside for 1 hour. Heat 2 tablespoons vegetable shortening in large skillet. Fry chops until well browned. In a separate skillet, heat 2 tablespoons vegetable shortening and fry potatoes until browned. Remove. Set aside and keep warm. Add remaining vegetable shortening to potato skillet and fry onions crisp. Add potatoes and onions to chops. Heat for 2 or 3 minutes. Serve with tomato sauce. Yield 4 to 5 servings

SPICED LAMB CHOPS AND VEGETABLES
[*Masalah Chop*]

3 tablespoons vegetable
  shortening
½ garlic clove, crushed
½ teaspoon ground ginger
⅛ teaspoon ground
  coriander
⅛ teaspoon mint leaves
Crushed red pepper to taste
¼ teaspoon ground cumin
2 teaspoons poppy seeds

½ teaspoon ground cinnamon
¼ teaspoon ground black
  pepper
Salt to taste
8 lamb chops, fat trimmed
1 large onion, thinly sliced
3 medium tomatoes, sliced
3 boiled potatoes, peeled and
  sliced

Heat vegetable shortening in large skillet. Fry all spices for 2 to 3 minutes. Add chops and fry until half cooked. Remove chops and keep warm. Add onion, tomatoes, and potatoes separately to skillet. Fry until browned. Remove vegetables and keep warm. Return chops to skillet and fry until browned. Serve chops with fried vegetables. *Yield* 4 to 5 servings

SPICED LAMB CHOPS
[*Bhap-Chop*]

1 garlic clove, crushed
½ teaspoon ground ginger
½ teaspoon ground coriander
¾ teaspoon ground cumin
Crushed red pepper to taste
Salt to taste
1¼ tablespoons vinegar

8 lamb chops, bone and
  fat removed
2 eggs, beaten
½ cup bread crumbs
3 tablespoons vegetable
  shortening

Combine garlic, ginger, coriander, cumin, red pepper, salt, and vinegar. Mix well. Rub chops with spice and set aside for 2 hours. Dip in egg and roll in bread crumbs. Heat vegetable shortening in large skillet. Fry until browned. Cover and cook until done. *Yield* 4 to 5 servings

LAMB CHOPS AND YOGURT
[*Dahi Chop*]

1½ cups yogurt
4 garlic cloves, crushed
1½ teaspoons ground ginger
¼ teaspoon ground coriander
Crushed red pepper to taste
½ teaspoon ground turmeric
10 peppercorns, ground

Salt to taste
8 lamb chops, fat trimmed
5 tablespoons vegetable
 shortening, divided
2 medium onions, thinly
 sliced

Place yogurt and spices in large mixing bowl. Mix well. Add chops and mix. Set aside for 1 hour. Heat 4 tablespoons vegetable shortening in large skillet. Fry chops and yogurt until brown and tender. Heat 1 tablespoon vegetable shortening in separate skillet. Fry onions until crisp. Garnish chops with crisp onions. *Yield* 4 to 5 servings

POTATO CAKES
[*Neeramish Chop*]

2 cups hot mashed potatoes
Salt and pepper to taste
Sugar to taste
5 tablespoons milk, divided
½ cup hot mashed peas
½ teaspoon ground ginger
¼ teaspoon ground cumin
2 teaspoons vinegar
¼ teaspoon chili powder

4 tablespoons vegetable
 shortening, divided
2 cloves
1 one-inch cinnamon stick
1 bay leaf
1 whole cardamom
4 tablespoons flour
4 tablespoons bread crumbs

Mix potatoes, salt, pepper, sugar, and 1 tablespoon of milk together in mixing bowl. Mix peas, ginger, cumin, vinegar, chili powder, salt, and sugar in another mixing bowl. Heat 1 tablespoon vegetable shortening in skillet. Add cloves, cinnamon, bay leaf, and cardamom. Fry 2 or 3 minutes. Add pea mixture and fry until light brown. Remove from heat and cool. Remove whole spices. Divide potatoes into 8 balls. Divide pea mixture in 8. Make a hole in each potato ball and stuff with pea mixture. Flatten each ball. Combine 4 tablespoons milk and flour to make a batter. Dip each potato cake in batter; coat lightly. Cover with bread crumbs. Heat 3 tablespoons vegetable shortening in skillet. Fry potato cakes until brown. *Yield* 8 cakes

BROILED KEBABS
[*Seekh Kebabs*]

*1 pound finely ground beef
  or lamb
1 egg
1 teaspoon ground cumin
Chili powder to taste
½ teaspoon ground cinnamon
4 cloves, crushed*

*Salt to taste
3 tablespoons vegetable
  shortening
1 lime, sliced
1 medium onion, sliced
1 large tomato, sliced*

Place meat, egg, and spices in mixing bowl. Mix well. Dampen fingers and make into 8 kebabs. Grease broiler pan with shortening and place kebabs in broiler. Baste with shortening. Broil kebabs until brown, turning with spatula. Garnish with onion, tomato, and lime. *Yield* 8 kebabs

SPICED MEAT KEBABS
[*Kabuli Kebabs*]

*1 large onion, quartered
½ teaspoon ground ginger
Crushed red pepper to taste
1 tablespoon grated coconut
¼ teaspoon ground coriander
¼ teaspoon ground cinnamon
4 cardamoms
8 almonds*

*Salt to taste
3 tablespoons vegetable
  shortening, divided
1 pound finely ground beef
  or lamb
2 tablespoons lentil or
  all-purpose flour*

Place onion, ginger, pepper, coconut, coriander, cinnamon, carda-moms, almonds, and salt in food chopper. Grind to a paste using fine blade or high-speed blender. Heat 1 teaspoon vegetable shortening in large skillet and add ground spices. Fry for 2 or 3 minutes. Add meat. Mix well, and fry slowly until meat is almost dry. Remove meat and form into small balls. Flatten balls out and coat with lentil flour. Heat 2 tablespoons of vegetable shortening in skillet and fry kebabs until brown. *Yield* 4 to 6 servings

BARBECUED BEEF OR LAMB SQUARES ON SKEWERS
[*Boti Kebabs*]

2 pounds sirloin steak or leg of lamb, cut in 1½-inch pieces	*1 teaspoons ground coriander*
	2 teaspoons ground turmeric
	2 teaspoons poppy seeds
Boiling water	*¼ teaspoon cayenne*
6 tablespoons yogurt	*2 teaspoons salt*
1 teaspoon ground ginger	*¼ cup vegetable shortening, melted*
¼ cup instant minced onion	

Soak meat in boiling water 5 minutes. Drain. Combine yogurt and seasonings to form a paste. Coat meat with paste and marinate at least 1 hour. String on skewers. Place under broiler or on a grill 7 to 10 minutes or until meat is cooked, basting well with melted shortening. Serve on skewers. If desired, squares of green pepper, tomato wedges, or mushrooms may be broiled with meat and alternated on the skewers. *Yield* 8 servings

BOTI KEBABS (cocktail size): Cut meat into 1-inch cubes. Marinate and cook, as in above directions, 5 to 7 minutes. String on toothpicks after broiling and serve with cocktails or at tea-time.

SPICED-MEAT PATE
[*Shami Kebabs*]

1 *pound ground round steak*
1 *cup hot water*
2 *teaspoons salt*
1 *two-inch cinnamon stick*
1 *whole ginger, 1½ inches long*
1 *teaspoon instant minced onion*
1 *teaspoon water*
¼ *teaspoon ground red pepper*
¼ *teaspoon ground cardamom*
1 *teaspoon ground black pepper*
¼ *teaspoon garlic powder*
½ *teaspoon finely crumbled mint flakes*
½ *cup chick-pea flour or corn meal, browned*
⅔ *cup water*
1 *tablespoon instant minced onion*
1 *tablespoon water*
1 *egg*
1 *tablespoon milk*
Vegetable shortening

Cook together, uncovered, in a saucepan, meat, 1 cup hot water, salt, cinnamon, and ginger 35 minutes or until all water has evaporated and the meat is very dry. Put meat in a strainer and press out all the excess fat. Soften instant minced onion in the 1 teaspoon water and add to the meat. Mix and put through a food chopper using the finest blade. Repeat to grind meat very fine. Add spices. Mix well. Cook chick-pea flour over medium heat in a saucepan or skillet until well browned (do not burn). Add to meat and mix well. Add the ⅔ cup water. Stir and cook over medium heat, about 5 minutes until meat holds together when squeezed. When cool enough to handle (about 5 minutes), shape 1 rounded tablespoon meat into a 2-inch patty. Soften remaining 1 tablespoon instant minced onion in the 1 tablespoon water. Place ¼ teaspoon in center of each patty. Pull meat over the onion until it is no longer visible. Beat together egg and milk. Dip meatballs in egg-milk mixture. Then roll in fine dry bread crumbs. Brown in deep vegetable shortening preheated to 375° F. Drain on paper towels. *Yield* 10 kebabs, each 2 inches in diameter

SPICED-MEAT KEBABS
[Nargisi Kebabs]

2 eggs
1 pound finely ground beef or
  lamb
¼ teaspoon ground ginger
½ teaspoon ground cumin
1 teaspoon ground coriander
½ teaspoon ground turmeric
Chili powder to taste

1 teaspoon ground cinnamon
4 cloves, ground
Salt to taste
8 hard-boiled eggs, shelled
3 tablespoons vegetable
  shortening
1½ tablespoons lime juice

Place raw eggs, meat, and spices in mixing bowl. Mix well. Dampen fingers and coat meat mixture on boiled eggs. Heat shortening in skillet and fry meat-covered eggs until brown. Sprinkle on lime juice and serve either whole or sliced lengthwise. *Yield* 8 kebabs

POTATO KEBABS
[Sabzi Kebabs]

1 cup mashed white potatoes
½ cup mashed sweet potatoes
4 slivers of garlic
¼ teaspoon ground ginger
¼ teaspoon coriander
Whole dry green or red pepper
  to taste

Salt to taste
½ teaspoon lime juice
Vegetable shortening for deep
  frying
½ fresh lime

Place mashed potatoes in mixing bowl. Grind to a paste the garlic, ginger, coriander, pepper, salt, and lime juice. Add spices to mashed potatoes and mix well. Divide into balls. Grease a wooden stick about ¼ inch thick or use pencil and wrap the balls around it with greased fingers. Gently slide off stick and deep-fry until brown. Sprinkle with juice from fresh lime. *Yield* 12 to 14 kebabs

POTATO AND PEA PATTIES
[*Vatanyachen Patties*]

6 tablespoons vegetable
   shortening, divided
¼ teaspoon mustard seeds
Crushed red peppers to taste
¼ teaspoon ground black
   pepper

1 cup cooked peas, mashed
1 cup mashed potatoes
½ coconut, grated
Salt to taste
½ cup rice flour

Heat 2 tablespoons shortening in skillet. Add mustard seeds, crushed red peppers, and pepper. Fry until mustard seeds burst. Place peas, potatoes, coconut, and salt in mixing bowl. Add fried spices. Mix well. Form small balls. Flatten into patties. Roll in rice flour. Heat 4 tablespoons of vegetable shortening in another skillet. Fry patties until golden brown. *Yield* 10 patties

SHRIMP CUTLETS
[*Chingrir Cutlet*]

2 medium onions
½ garlic clove
¾ teaspoon ground ginger
Crushed red peppers to taste
8 large shrimp

1 egg, beaten
½ cup bread crumbs
4 tablespoons vegetable
   shortening

Place onions, garlic, ginger, and crushed red peppers in food chopper. Use fine blade or high-speed blender. Grind to a paste. Slit shrimp lengthwise and make light gashes on the surface. Smear shrimp with paste. Allow to stand ½ hour. Dip shrimp in egg. Cover with bread crumbs. Heat vegetable shortening in skillet. Fry shrimp until crisp and brown. *Yield* 2 servings

FISH CAKES
[*Muchlee Shifta*]

3 cups cooked flaked fish
4 medium onions, quartered
½ teaspoon ground turmeric
3 garlic cloves
4 tablespoons chopped
  parsley
1 tablespoon chopped mint
Salt and pepper to taste
½ teaspoon ground ginger

1½ teaspoons vegetable oil
½ cup chick-pea or all-
  purpose flour
Salt to taste
Cayenne to taste
1 teaspoon ground cumin
Vegetable shortening for
  frying

Grind together in food chopper the fish, onions, turmeric, garlic, parsley, mint, salt, pepper, and ginger. Place in mixing bowl. Mix well. Add vegetable oil. Make into long egg-shape cakes. Combine chick-pea flour, salt, cayenne, and cumin. Roll fish cakes in seasoned flour. Set aside for 15 to 20 minutes. Heat shortening in skillet and fry fish cakes. *Yield* 4 to 6 servings

STEAK
[*Pasande*]

¼ cup chick-pea or all-
  purpose flour
1 teaspoon ground allspice
½ teaspoon ground nutmeg
4 garlic cloves, crushed

¼ cup grated onion
1 teaspoon salt
Chili powder to taste
4 minute steaks, thinly cut

Blend together, chick-pea flour, allspice, nutmeg, garlic, onions, salt, and chili powder. Rub into steaks. Lay steaks flat one on top of the other. Place a heavy weight or skillet on top of steaks so that steaks will flatten out and seasonings will penetrate. Allow to stand for 1 or 2 hours. Heat shortening in large skillet and fry rare, medium, or well done. *Yield* 4 servings

Part II
OTHER SPECIALTIES
FROM INDIA

Festivals of India

This is a time of overflowing harvest. A time to salute the sun on its entry into Capricorn after one has faithfully tended the winter crops. A time to thank God who made light and water which causes foods to grow. That is "Pongal." The rice, millet, or cotton will be sold. There will be money to take a wife or negotiate a marriage for a daughter. But first there must be celebrations for fifteen days. For breakfast on each of these mornings there will be different combinations in flavor and texture of rice, wheat, or lentils. Appropriately, the first day of the festival begins on the farm, near the cattle pen. The boys have washed each bull, cow, and sheep with a hard brush and fragrant roots. The horns are painted with bright paint. The coats bear the imprint of hands in blue, red, and green. They all wear a headband of black and red beads made by the shepherds.

In a new pot, decorated with lime paste and fresh turmeric, *Payasam* is a delicious pudding of newly pounded rice, sugar-cane juice, milk, black peppers, a suggestion of camphor, a handful of green gram (split peas), and tiny specks of bright, golden, new turmeric, is made. This is scooped up in ladlefuls. First the cattle are fed as a symbolic gesture of veneration, then the shepherds partake while other farmhands take a stick of sugar cane in one hand and beat on a brass plate, marching around the field shouting "*Pongalo-Pongal*" (it's brimming full).

This is one of the biggest festivals in the state of Madras, Mysore, and Andhra Pradesh. In some cities in Madras the climax of the festivities is a version of the bullfight when unarmed youths try to wrest away bundles of money which have been tied to the horns of the ferocious bulls.

In Andhra Pradesh the most exciting part of the community festival is the bullock race to which several villages send their select teams in the hope of capturing the much-coveted prizes. Cockfights are held in most villages.

ID-UL FITAR (Ramzan-Id)
[*February 26*]

Id Mubarak, meaning to say, "Congratulations, the month of fasting is over! Many happy returns!" After the rigors of the month of Ramzan, every Muslim now rejoices; all wear their best new clothes; all pray in the mosque, row upon row, prince touching shoulders with pauper; after worship comes time for feasting and time for charities.

Trays of *halwas* topped with gold or silver foil and then covered with a white lace cloth will be sent to the homes of friends and benefactors, wishing *Id Mubarak*. At home, the family will sit around an enormous platter, heaped with *biriyani* cooked with the choicest meat. All delve into the same dish. Why not? Are we not all brothers?

Considering India was almost completely vegetarian at the time of the Muslim invasion, it is noteworthy that these "foreigners" succeeded in teaching Hindus and Buddhists, not only to relish meat but to add to it the use of their own famed spices (garlic, sweet spices, dry ginger, asafetida) to develop what is today an elaborate cooking tradition.

JANAMASTAMI
[*August 12*]

Now comes Janamastami, the birthday of the shepherd god "Krishna"—darling of the *gopis*, (milkmaids). Krishna's home is in Kathiawar. And here in particular the cattle owners consider

this their chief festival. On this day the people simulate the be-
loved pranks of the boy god (such as climbing up the ladders of
his mother's friends' homes to steal butter, hiding their clothes,
etc.). The former idea of simulated pranks has developed into a
ceremonious, wildly exciting game among young fellows. On the
day previous to Janamastami a mud pot is chosen. Into this, donors
of the area put whatever amount of money they wish to contrib-
ute as a birthday tribute to Krishna. The pot is closed with a
coconut and the stopper is secured. The entire thing is hung high
on the branch of a tree or the ledge of a building—the higher the
riskier, the better and more meritorious. On Janamastami day the
boys of the neighborhood climb one on top of the other to form
a human pillar. To build a steady one generally takes several
hours of perspiring perseverance. When the boys have reached the
top where the pot hangs, it is broken so as to scatter the money
which is collected by the boys. With their booty they buy food
and, singing the praise of Krishna, they go to the sea to bathe before feasting. Their action symbolizes the act of working hard for
the good things in life, then sharing with all.

The *halwa* sweets made at this season are cooked with the mis-
chievous shepherd boy Krishna in mind who loved crunchy sweets
and yummy milk puddings.

ONAM
[August 31 to September 3]

This is the greatest festival of Kerala. It is primarily a harvest
celebration and marks the end of the monsoons. The Earth has
been washed clean. People can now emerge from under their
palm-frond umbrellas. For them this has been a period of hiber-
nation. Now they must work: on the sea front men return to put
out their fishing boats—and on the farms the men take up their
tasks. This festival is observed not only in the homes but out in
the open against a backdrop of lush green tropical vegetation and
palm-fringed lagoons.

The most spectacular part of the festival is the Snake Boat Races which take place in many communities. Different kinds of boats—beak-shaped, kite-tailed, curly-headed—take part in contests in which the boats are rowed to powerful rhythmic music.

The approach of this festival is announced first by the kitchen aromas. Usually there is the smell of rice flour being cooked in boiling *jaggery* (molasses); one dish is called Parthaman.

The house fronts are freshly washed and plastered and covered with patterns which the girls have traced symbolizing festive hospitality; the rose-water sprinkler, the bowl which holds the sandalwood paste; and the plate or *thali* for fruit and coconut.

During this festival in some places a special main dish is eaten which is made of equal quantities of all types of beans, freshly taken from the pods and mildly flavored. This delicacy is substantial enough to have sustained, in the olden and in present days, the husbands and fathers who went forth on their first outing to the fields after the many weeks of inactivity brought about by the too heavy rains.

DASARA
[September 18 to 28]

Come the middle of September the country will enter into a festival mood. The entire peninsula, from its southernmost tip punctuating the confluence of the three great seas to the smallest hamlet high in the Himalayas, young and old, rich and poor put aside their cares and break the humdrum routine for ten days to celebrate the most popular and longest of India's festivals.

Although there are regional variations with emphasis on a particular deity popular in a specific area, the central theme of Dasara, the festival of ten nights, is the same throughout the country—the triumph of good over evil.

Each province will hold its celebrations in its own individual way. In a far-off village in the tiger-ridden mountains, people come with their blankets to sit through chilly nights in open-air theater galleries hewn out of the mountainside. They will watch a shadow play of the religious epic, Ramayana, extolling the exploits of the hero Rama. In the capital, huge pasteboard effigies of Ravana, the Wise Giant, will be burned. The Goddess Parvati is especially remembered in Bengal. In Mysore the Maharaja organizes colorful pageantry. All over South India, mothers take out their childhood toys and dress them in new silks and tinsel. They grow small fields on trays with mud and seedlings, making hills and rivers, and these are arranged on the ten steps of the tableau depicting Dasara.

Everywhere women visit one another and treats are served, such as Usal or Dal Mote; boiled, spiced chick-peas tossed in coconut; a dry mix of sweet spices, sugar, chick-pea flour and chopped nuts; plantains; betel nuts; and *pedha*.

All grown-up girls and young mothers are looked upon with special favor as they symbolize, during this season, the other side of Parvati who, besides being a dread goddess when angered, is also a tender human girl who hates to leave home after her annual visit with her parents.

DIVALI (Festival of Light)
[October 16 and 17]

Divali occurs a fortnight after Dasara. It is celebrated on the dark night before the bright full moon and it seems fitting to pray "Lead us from darkness to light . . . lead us from death to immortality." The spirit of this festival is enhanced because this is also the time when Lakshmi will visit every home in India; Lakshmi, the goddess of wealth and prosperity!

On the first night it is customary for all to fast so that on the next night, the Festival of Light, they can diligently cancel all darkness with bright fireworks to show the way to Lakshmi.

Before the feasting, all Hindus indulge in a sumptuous ceremonial oil bath. Specially medicated oils are rubbed on head and body and then removed with a mixture of ground grain, sandalwood, khuskhus roots, and fragrant herbs. All are later washed off with tanks of hot water. For some reason the new sons-in-law receive all the attention. They are pampered with the choicest foods such as *Subh Degh* and new clothes. The poor water carrier who has worked all night filling the baths receives a coin from each bather which is left in the water and collected by him before he refills the bath again.

In the remote corners of the land where expensive fireworks are not sold, original games of torch spinning are still played. Boys make torches with oiled rags on the end of a bamboo stick. These they light and spin around repeating a song: "My spark enters your torch, yours, mine. The torch is cosmos, sparks, you or I. We'll spark again from elsewhere, why die?"

INDIAN CHRISTMAS

In spite of the lack of snow, the Christmas spirit holds sway every December in India. Christians, Hindus, or Moslems, are all in the mood for having as good a time as they do during the celebrations of Id or Divali.

It is not unusual to see Hindu and Christian friends shopping together as early as October; one shops for new clothes for Divali while the other shops for Christmas, packing these things away until December 25. The shops are more fully stocked in October because of Dasara and the coming of Divali and Christmas. Dry fruits are cheaper, and there is a larger selection of everything.

The custom of eating cakes such as *Sooji* cake at Christmas has become as much a part of Indian life as *pedha* at Divali and Dasara.

In Christian homes a touching ceremony is acted out when the cake is being mixed. The oldest member of the house is assigned the duty of adding the mixed fruit into the batter. This he does with a special scoop. Each scoopful is put in, in the name of a member of the family. New additions are given first place. As years advance, one can imagine Grandfather having quite a time keeping count of all the names so as not to miss out on anyone.

The cake is cut only after it is blessed on Christmas morning. This gracious custom is part of ancient Indian culture.

Churches are overflowing. If it is in the North, men will be "booted and suited" as the saying goes. It will be bitterly cold. In the South, worshipers leave their sandals at the steps of the church. But women everywhere will be smelling of new silks, fruit cake, and a faint aroma of onion for they will all have been busy in the kitchen up until the last minute endowing the ancient recipes, such as Anarse or Buffado, borrowed from the early Christian settlers, with a very special oriental extravagance.

Breads —
Roti, Poori, and Paratha

FRIED BREAD PUFFS
[Pooris]

2 cups sifted all-purpose
  flour
1 teaspoon salt
¼ cup vegetable shortening

6 tablespoons water
Vegetable shortening for
  deep frying

Sift together 2 cups all-purpose flour and salt into a mixing bowl.
Melt ¼ cup vegetable shortening and mix well with the flour. Stir
in water, mixing thoroughly with the hands. Knead dough 5 to 7
minutes, pressing down hard with the knuckles until dough has a
satiny appearance. Or, put dough through a food chopper 8 to 10
times, using the medium blade (this method saves time and results are excellent). Roll dough very thin on pastry board. Cut
into 3-inch circles. Drop each into deep vegetable shortening preheated to 360° F. As soon as dough begins to puff, which is about
½ minute, press the pooris lightly with perforated pancake turner.
Turn to brown lightly on the other side. Pooris cook quickly, re-
quiring only about 1 minute cooking time. Drain on paper towel.
Serve hot when possible. Yield about 16 pooris

FOR COCKTAIL SIZE: Cut the above dough in 1½-inch circles, fry
and sprinkle with seasoning salt as soon as they are removed from
shortening.

LENTIL-FILLED PANCAKES
[*Dal Pooris*]

2 tablespoons vegetable
  shortening, divided
1 tablespoon ground cumin
  seeds
1 cardamom, finely ground
4 cloves, finely ground
1 one-inch cinnamon stick,
  finely ground

Whole dry red pepper, ground
  to taste
1 cup lentils, soaked
Salt to taste
1 cup sifted whole-wheat flour
Vegetable shortening for deep
  frying

Heat 1 tablespoon vegetable shortening and fry ground spices slowly. Grind lentils to a paste in food chopper using fine blade or high-speed blender. Add lentil paste to spices and mix. Fry spices and lentil paste until all moisture is absorbed. Rub 1 tablespoon of vegetable shortening into the flour and knead to a soft dough. Divide dough into 8 balls. Press each ball in the center and fill with fried spices and lentil paste. Close the opening well and flatten. Roll out into rounds about 4 inches in diameter. Deep-fry in vegetable shortening on slow heat. *Yield 8 pooris*

PANCAKE BREAD
[*Paratha*]

2 tablespoons vegetable
  shortening, divided

2 cups whole-wheat flour
Pinch of salt

Blend 2 tablespoons of shortening into 2 cups flour and salt and make a soft dough. Divide into two balls and roll out evenly into big rounds. Smear each with shortening, sprinkle with flour, and form into a roll. Cut into about 2-inch pieces. Place each piece cut side up, flatten and roll very thin to pancake size. Lightly grease griddle and fry each *paratha* on both sides until crisp and evenly brown. Serve hot. *Yield* 6 to 8 servings

Note: For more flakiness, smear the round with shortening, fold in half, smear again with shortening, fold over to form the shape of a cone. Roll out and fry.

STUFFED PANCAKE BREAD
[*Mooli Ka Paratha*]

2 *teaspoons vegetable shortening*	*Salt to taste*
½ *cup whole-wheat flour*	4 *medium radishes, finely grated*

Blend 2 teaspoons of shortening into flour and salt. Knead and prepare dough. Divide into 8 balls and roll out very thin to pancake size. Spread ¼ of grated radish on one round and cover with another round; press down edges. Lightly grease griddle and fry *paratha* on both sides until crisp and brown. Serve with yogurt or sweet butter. *Yield* 4 *parathas*

Note: Mashed potatoes, chopped cooked cauliflower, cooked and mashed peas may be used for stuffing *parathas*.

LAMB-STUFFED PANCAKE
[*Queema Paratha*]

2 *cups whole-wheat flour*	1 *pound finely ground lamb*
½ *teaspoon salt*	¼ *teaspoon ground turmeric*
1 *tablespoon butter or margarine*	*Chili powder to taste*
6 *tablespoons vegetable shortening, divided*	¼ *teaspoon ground black pepper*
1 *medium onion, finely chopped*	1 *teaspoon ground cinnamon*
	Salt to taste

Sift together flour and salt. Rub 1 tablespoon butter or margarine into flour and knead to a soft dough. Use a little water if necessary.

Divide dough into 12 balls. Roll out like pancakes. Reserve. Heat 1 tablespoon vegetable shortening in skillet. Add onion. Fry until light brown. Add meat, turmeric, chili powder, pepper, cinnamon, and salt. Fry for 6 minutes. Set aside and allow to cool. Divide meat in 6 portions. Spread 1 portion of meat mixture on each *paratha*. Cover with another *paratha*. Press edges well. Heat remaining vegetable shortening in skillet. Fry filled *paratha* slowly until brown and crisp. *Yield* 6 *parathas*

PANCAKE BREAD
[*Phulka*]

2 *cups whole-wheat flour*
Salt to taste
Water

Mix salt and flour together and add just enough water to make a soft dough. Set the dough aside for a half hour. Knead again thoroughly and form into small balls. Roll out paper thin on board to pancakes about 5 inches in diameter. Place *phulkas* on ungreased griddle until done on one side then turn over until done. Remove from griddle. Spread on a little butter or margarine and serve hot. *Yield* 8 to 10 servings

BAKED GRIDDLE CAKE
[*Roghni Roti*]

2 *cups sifted all-purpose flour*   3 *tablespoons milk*
¼ *teaspoon salt*   *Water*
2 *tablespoons vegetable*
  shortening

Sift together flour and salt. Rub shortening in the flour and knead to a soft dough with milk and a little water if necessary. Roll out about ¼ inch thick and place on warm griddle over low heat. Bake until crisp and brown on both sides. *Yield* 3 to 4 *rotis*

SPICED PANCAKE BREAD
[Besani Roti]

½ cup lentil or chick-pea
  flour
¾ cup whole-wheat flour
Crushed red peppers to taste
1 medium onion, finely
  chopped

¼ teaspoon ground coriander
Salt to taste
2 tablespoons vegetable
  shortening

Combine all ingredients except vegetable shortening. Knead, adding just enough water to make a soft dough. Divide into 12 small balls. Roll out like thin pancake. Heat vegetable shortening on griddle or in large skillet. Fry *roti* evenly on both sides. *Yield* 12 *rotis*

GRIDDLE BREAD
[Ma Poli]

2 cups sifted rice flour
2 cups boiling water
Salt or sugar to taste
1 tablespoon vegetable
  shortening
1 cup sifted all-purpose flour

1 cup water
1 teaspoon ground cardamom
Salt to taste
1 tablespoon vegetable
  shortening

Combine rice flour, boiling water, salt, and vegetable shortening. Knead to form a soft dough. Turn out on greased board. Form into small balls. Combine flour, water, cardamom, and salt. Knead to a soft dough. Grease hands. Take a little of the second dough and flatten it. Place a dough ball in the center. Pull flat dough around ball to fully cover. Repeat until all dough balls are used. Flatten and roll out each covered dough ball to look like a *chapati*. Heat shortening in skillet. Fry *poli* until both sides are golden brown. *Yield* 12 *ma poli*

THREE-LAYER GRIDDLE BREAD
[*Teen Padari Poli*]

1 cup sifted whole-wheat flour	¼ cup milk
Salt to taste	Butter or margarine
½ tablespoon vegetable shortening	Vegetable shortening for frying

Sift together flour and salt. Place flour in mixing bowl. Rub ½ tablespoon of vegetable shortening into flour and knead with milk to a soft dough. Divide into 3 equal portions. Roll out each portion into a thin pancake. Smear one pancake with butter or margarine, sprinkle with dry flour, place another one on top of it. Smear again with butter or margarine, sprinkle with flour, place third pancake on it. Heat vegetable shortening in large skillet. Shallow- fry. *Yield* 4 servings

STUFFED GRIDDLE CAKES
[*Ratalyachi Poli*]

1 cup sifted whole-wheat flour	½ teaspoon ground cardamom
¼ cup water	2 tablespoons sugar
1 cup mashed sweet potatoes	Vegetable shortening

Place flour in mixing bowl. Add a little water at a time, kneading flour to a soft dough. Divide into 4 balls. In another bowl mix together the sweet potatoes, cardamoms, and sugar. Divide into 4 portions. Make a hole in each flour ball and fill with one sweet-potato ball. Roll like a *chapati*. Grease griddle or a skillet. Fry on both sides until brown. *Yield* 4 *polis*

PEA-FILLED PANCAKES
[*Karaishutir Kochuri*]

3 *tablespoons vegetable shortening, divided*
1½ *cups sifted flour*
½ *cup cooked peas, mashed*
¾ *teaspoon ground ginger*

Crushed red peppers to taste
2 *teaspoons anise seeds*
Salt to taste
Vegetable shortening for deep frying

Rub 2 tablespoons of vegetable shortening in flour and knead to a soft dough. Mash together peas, ginger, crushed red peppers, and anise seeds. Heat 1 tablespoon of vegetable shortening in skillet. Add mashed-pea mixture and salt. Fry 2 or 3 minutes. Remove from heat and allow to cool. Divide dough into 8 balls. Press each ball in the center and fill with pea mixture. Close opening and flatten. Roll out to pancake shape. Heat vegetable shortening in skillet. Deep-fry each *kochuri* until brown. *Yield* 8 *kochuris*

CRISP LENTIL BALLS
[*Khasta Kachauri*]

½ *cup lentils, soaked overnight*
¼ *teaspoon chili powder*
1 *teaspoon ground cumin*
1 *teaspoon ground ginger*
Salt to taste

2 *cups all-purpose flour*
3 *tablespoons vegetable shortening*
Vegetable shortening for deep frying

Place lentils in food chopper. Use fine blade or high-speed blender. Grind to a paste. Add chili power, cumin, ginger, and salt. Mix well. Divide into 20 small balls. Place flour in mixing bowl. Rub in 3 tablespoons vegetable shortening. Knead to a soft dough. Divide into 20 small balls. Make a dent in each flour ball. Fill with paste ball. Close up. Flatten into cutlet shapes. Heat vegetable shortening for deep frying in large skillet. Deep-fry balls until brown. *Yield* 20 *kachauris*

LENTIL KNISHES
[*Kusta Kutchori*]

½ cup lentils   1 cup yogurt
½ teaspoon chili powder   Vegetable shortening for
4½ cups whole-wheat flour   deep frying
½ cup vegetable shortening

Soak lentils in warm water 1 inch above lentils. Place soaked
lentils in food chopper. Use fine blade. Grind to paste. Add chili
powder. Mix well. Place flour in mixing bowl. Rub in shortening.
Add yogurt. Knead to a stiff dough. Cover. Set aside for ½
hour. Divide dough into balls the size of small lemon. Press center
with thumb to make a small hollow. Fill with lentil paste. Close
up filled hollow. Place ball on floured board. Roll into a disc 2½
inches in diameter. Heat vegetable shortening for deep frying in
skillet. Deep-fry until brown. *Yield* 2½ to 3 dozen

Soups and Lentils

DRY LENTILS
[Sookhi Dal]

½ cup lentils
1 tablespoon vegetable
  shortening
4 slivers of garlic

Whole dry green or red
  pepper, chopped, to taste
1 teaspoon ground turmeric
1½ teaspoons cumin seeds
Salt to taste

Soak lentils for an hour, drain the water. Heat shortening in skillet. Add garlic, chopped pepper, turmeric, and cumin. Add lentils and fry for 5 minutes. Sprinkle lentils with a little water, cover them up and cook on low heat till tender. Add salt and stir, approximately 1 hour. *Yield* 4 to 6 servings

LENTILS, POTATOES, AND TOMATOES
[Dhonkar Dalna]

1 cup lentils, soak overnight
1 medium onion, quartered
1¼ teaspoons ground ginger
4 tablespoons vegetable
  shortening, divided
1 teaspoon ground cumin
Crushed red peppers to taste
½ teaspoon ground turmeric
Salt to taste

1 medium onion, finely sliced
2 large tomatoes, quartered
2 large potatoes, cubed
Sugar to taste
2 cloves, crushed
⅛ teaspoon ground cardamom
1 teaspoon ground cinnamon
2 teaspoons water

Place lentils in food chopper. Use fine blade or high-speed blender and grind to a paste. Reserve. Place quartered onion and ginger in food chopper or blender and grind to a paste. Heat 1 teaspoon of vegetable shortening in skillet. Add lentil paste, onion, and ginger paste, cumin, crushed red peppers, turmeric, and salt. Fry until dry. Remove and spread mixture on a plate. Cool and cut in 1½-inch cubes. Heat 1 teaspoon of vegetable shortening in skillet. Add cubes. Fry until light brown. Drain and reserve. Heat 3 tablespoons vegetable shortening. Add sliced onions. Fry until brown. Add tomatoes. Fry slowly for 5 minutes. Add potatoes, salt, sugar, and enough water to cook potatoes. Add lentil cubes when potatoes are almost cooked. Combine cloves, cardamom, cinnamon, 2 teaspoons water, and mix. Add to skillet. Mix well. Remove. *Yield* 4 servings

LENTILS AND POTATOES
[*Shakkariyan Ni Dal*]

½ cup lentils, wash and soak
  2 hours
4 cups water
1 large sweet potato, peeled
  and cubed
1½ tablespoons vegetable
  shortening

½ cup unsweetened cooked
  rhubarb
1 teaspoon ground turmeric
1¼ teaspoons ground ginger
Crushed red peppers to taste
1 tablespoon brown sugar
Salt to taste

Place lentils and water in pan. Bring to a boil. Add sweet potato and cook until soft, approximately 1 hour. Heat vegetable shortening in small skillet. Add rhubarb, turmeric, ginger, crushed red peppers, brown sugar, and salt. Fry for 3 or 4 minutes. Add to lentils and sweet potatoes. Mash to a pulp. Serve hot. *Yield* 4 servings

TOMATO AND LENTILS
[*Tomatochen Sar*]

1 medium tomato, quartered
½ cup lentils
4 cups water
½ garlic clove, crushed
¾ teaspoon ground ginger
¼ teaspoon ground coriander
1 tablespoon vegetable
shortening

Crushed red peppers to taste
¼ teaspoon mustard seeds
¼ teaspoon ground cumin
⅛ teaspoon curry powder
¼ teaspoon ground turmeric
Salt to taste

Place tomatoes, lentils, and water in pan. Bring to a boil. Cook until lentils are soft, approximately 1 hour. Pour and mash through a strainer into bowl. Add garlic, ginger, and coriander. Mix well. Heat vegetable shortening. Add crushed red peppers, mustard seeds, cumin, and curry powder. Fry until mustard seeds burst. Add turmeric, tomato-and-lentil mixture and salt. Bring to a boil. Remove. *Yield* 4 servings

SPICED LENTILS
[*Vendhaiya Sambar*]

1 cup lentils, soaked 3 to 4
hours
½ teaspoon fenugreek seeds
3 tablespoons grated coconut
2½ teaspoons ground cumin
seeds
4 teaspoons ground black
pepper
1 teaspoon ground cinnamon
1 cup rhubarb juice,
unsweetened

Salt to taste
1 teaspoon brown sugar
Chili powder to taste
1 teaspoon ground coriander
¼ cup vegetable shortening
1½ teaspoons ground mustard
½ teaspoon crushed red
pepper
1 teaspoon ground turmeric
1 garlic clove, crushed

Cook lentils and fenugreek seeds in water to cover until soft, approximately 1½ hours. Grind to a paste: coconut, cumin, and cinnamon in food chopper using fine blade or high-speed blender. Boil together rhubarb juice, salt, brown sugar, chili powder, and coriander for 5 minutes. Heat shortening in skillet. Add mustard, pepper, turmeric, and garlic. Fry for 5 minutes. Add to lentils with same spoon. Mix well. Add spiced rhubarb juice to lentils and bring to a boil. Serve. *Yield* 4 servings

CURRIED POTATO SOUP
[*Aloo Shoorva*]

3 cups diced raw potatoes
2½ cups boiling water
3 chicken or beef bouillon
　cubes
¾ teaspoon salt
2 garlic cloves, minced
1¾ teaspoons curry powder

¾ cup chopped onion
2 cups milk
2 tablespoons butter or
　margarine
¼ teaspoon ground black
　pepper

Combine potatoes, water, bouillon cubes, salt, garlic, curry powder, and onion. Cover and cook until potatoes fall apart, 40–50 minutes. Remove from heat and mash potatoes in the liquid. If necessary put mixture through a sieve. Add milk, butter or margarine, and black pepper. Heat only until hot. *Yield* 5 cups or 6 servings

LENTIL SOUP
[*Dal Soup*]

1 cup lentils
2 cloves garlic
Pinch turmeric
4 cups water
¼ onion, chopped

1 teaspoon vegetable
　shortening
Salt to taste
2 tablespoons heavy cream

Simmer lentils with garlic and turmeric in water until lentils are soft, approximately 1½ hours. Strain; reserve liquid. Mash lentils to make a thick purée. Add reserved liquid. Sauté onion in shortening until brown and crisp. Add lentil mixture and salt. Reheat. Before serving, stir in cream. *Yield* 4 servings

LIME SOUP
[*Lime Rasam*]

4 cups boiling water	1 garlic clove, crushed
1 teaspoon freshly ground black pepper	¼ cup chopped Chinese parsley
1 teaspoon brown sugar	½ cup lime juice
1 teaspoon salt	

Add pepper, sugar, salt, and garlic to boiling water. Add parsley. Cook for 5 minutes. Add lime juice. Remove from heat. Steep for 1 hour. Strain. Serve hot or cold. *Yield* 4 servings

CUMIN SOUP
[*Cumin Rasam*]

2 tablespoons cumin seeds	½ teaspoon cayenne
4 cups water	Pulp of small lemon
1 teaspoon freshly ground black pepper	2 teaspoons coriander seeds
	Salt to taste

Add cumin to water. Set aside in warm place overnight. Strain. Reserve water. Reserve cumin. Place soaked cumin, pepper, cayenne, lemon pulp, coriander, and ½ cup cumin water in high-speed blender. Blend for 2 or 3 minutes. Pour in saucepan. Boil for 5 minutes. Add remaining cumin water. Remove from heat. Add salt to taste. Steep for 1 hour. Strain. Serve hot or cold. *Yield* 4 servings

BEET SOUP
[Beet Rasam]

1 cup cooked diced beets
2 cups boiling water, divided
1 large onion, chopped
4 cloves
1 one-inch stick of cinnamon

8 peppercorns
3 tablespoons lentils
Salt to taste
½ tablespoon lemon juice

Place beets in wooden bowl and add 1 cup boiling water. Mash beets with wooden spoon. Strain through a coarse sieve. In a separate pan, boil onion, cloves, cinnamon, peppercorns, lentils, and salt in 1 cup of boiling water until thick. Mash well. Add lemon juice and mix well. Add beet juice. *Yield* 4 servings

GINGER SOUP
[Ginger Rasam]

3 cups boiling water
3 teaspoons ground ginger,
    divided
¼ cup lime juice

2 tablespoons honey
½ teaspoon freshly ground
    black pepper

Add 2½ teaspoons ginger to boiling water. Reduce heat. Simmer 5 minutes. Add remaining ingredients. Serve hot with rice. *Yield* 4 servings

SPICED YOGURT
[*Takachi Kadhi*]

1 tablespoon vegetable
 shortening
¼ teaspoon mustard seeds
¼ teaspoon curry powder
1 cup yogurt
2 tablespoons lentil or chick-
 pea flour

Crushed red peppers to taste
1 garlic clove, crushed
¼ teaspoon ground coriander
1¼ teaspoons ground ginger
Salt to taste

Heat vegetable shortening in skillet. Add mustard seeds and curry powder. Fry until mustard seeds burst. Add yogurt, lentil flour, crushed red peppers, garlic, coriander, ginger, and salt. Cook for 5 minutes. *Yield* 4 servings

Chutneys, Pickles, Pachadis, and Raitas

BENGAL CHUTNEY

1 cup raisins
1¼ teaspoons ground ginger
6 garlic cloves

½ teaspoon hot-pepper
sauce
1 teaspoon salt
1 tablespoon vinegar

Place all ingredients in food chopper. Use fine blade or high-speed blender. Grind smooth. *Yield* 1 cup

PARSLEY CHUTNEY

1 cup chopped parsley
6 garlic cloves
1¼ teaspoons ground ginger
¼ teaspoon crushed red
pepper

1 tablespoon lemon pulp
1 tablespoon brown sugar
1 teaspoon salt
Yogurt

Place all ingredients except yogurt in food chopper. Use fine blade or high-speed blender. Grind smooth. Add just enough yogurt to make mixture pouring batter consistency. Beat smooth. *Yield* 2 cups

Note: The above recipe made with the same amount of coriander leaves, in place of parsley, is an all-India favorite chutney.

CHUTNEY FOR DOSAIS OR IDLIES

½ coconut, grated
Crushed red pepper to taste
1¼ teaspoons ground ginger
2 teaspoons finely chopped
   onion

1 tablespoon lime juice
Salt to taste
2 teaspoons vegetable
   shortening
½ teaspoon mustard seeds

Place coconut, pepper, ginger, and onion in food chopper; grind to a paste using fine blade or high-speed blender. Add lime juice and salt. Heat vegetable shortening in skillet. Add mustard seeds. Fry until seeds burst. Add coconut paste. Stir well and remove from heat. Serve with *dosais* or *idlies*. Yield ½ to 1 cup of chutney

Note: ½ cup yogurt may be added to chutney after removing from heat.

RHUBARB CHUTNEY

2 pounds rhubarb, washed
2 peeled lemons
2 cups sugar
2 cups white vinegar

1½ cups raisins
2 tablespoons salt
2 tablespoons crushed garlic
2 one-inch pieces of ginger

Dice rhubarb very fine. Chop lemon pulp and remove white skin membranes. Place rhubarb, lemon, and remaining ingredients in kettle. Boil until mixture becomes very thick. Remove ginger. Pour chutney in a jar. Cover tightly. Keep for one month before using. Yield 1 quart

MINT CHUTNEY

1 cup fresh chopped mint
6 garlic cloves
2 tablespoons sugar
1¼ teaspoons ground ginger

¼ cup vinegar
1 teaspoon salt
1 tablespoon grated coconut

Place all ingredients in food chopper; use fine blade or high-speed blender. Grind smooth. Yield 1¼ cups

GREEN-TOMATO CHUTNEY

2 *pounds green tomatoes,* 2 *tablespoons ground cloves*
 peeled and sliced 4 *cups brown sugar*
4 *tablespoons ground mustard* 1½ *cups white vinegar*
2 *tablespoons ground* ¼ *teaspoon cayenne*
 cinnamon

Combine all ingredients in kettle. Boil until thick. Pour chutney into jar. Cool. Cover tightly. Keep for 2 or 3 weeks before using. *Yield* 1 quart

Note: Apples may be substituted for tomatoes.

BANANA AND YOGURT
[*Kelanu Raitun*]

1 *teaspoon vegetable* 1 *cup yogurt*
 shortening *Chili powder to taste*
1 *teaspoon cumin seeds* *Salt to taste*
2 *large soft bananas, mashed*

Heat vegetable shortening in skillet. Add cumin seeds. Fry 2 or 3 minutes. Remove from heat. Stir in bananas, yogurt, chili powder, and salt. *Yield* 4 servings

ONION AND RADISH RELISH
[*Peaz Ka Lachha*]

1½ *cups finely chopped* ½ *teaspoon salt or salt to*
 onion *taste*
¼ *cup finely chopped green* ⅛ *teaspoon cayenne*
 pepper 2 *teaspoons fresh lemon juice*
3 *tablespoons coarsely* *or lemon juice to taste*
 chopped radishes *Paprika*

Combine onion, green pepper, radishes, salt, cayenne, and lemon juice. Mix well. Garnish with paprika. Serve as a relish with curries. *Yield* 6 servings

SPICED RELISH
[*Tamboli*]

1 tablespoon vegetable
   shortening
⅛ teaspoon curry powder
¼ teaspoon mustard seeds
1½ teaspoons coriander
   seeds, finely ground, divided
¼ teaspoon mustard seeds,
   finely ground

¼ teaspoon cumin seeds,
   finely ground
4 peppercorns, finely ground
Chili powder to taste
4 tablespoons lemon juice
1 large onion, finely chopped
1 cup grated coconut
Salt to taste
Sugar to taste

Heat vegetable shortening, add curry and ¼ teaspoon mustard
seeds. When mustard seeds burst, add 1 teaspoon coriander,
ground mustard seeds, cumin, peppercorns, and chili powder.
Blend well and fry for 2 minutes. Add lemon juice. Mix well.
Add onion, ½ teaspoon coriander, coconut, salt, and sugar. Mix
well. *Yield* 4 servings

CARROT AND ONION SALAD
[*Gajur Peaz Sambal*]

2 teaspoons salt
1 teaspoon ground turmeric
1 teaspoon powdered mustard
½ teaspoon chili powder

2 teaspoons sugar
1 large onion, thinly sliced
1 cup shredded carrots
¼ cup thinly sliced limes

Mix together salt, turmeric, mustard, chili, and sugar. Place
onion, carrots, and lime slices in salad bowl. Add mixed spices.
Toss as for salad. *Yield* 4 servings

COCONUT SAUCE
[*Nariul Thovayal*]

1 cup grated coconut
1 tablespoon ground ginger
1 teaspoon salt
1 tablespoon lemon pulp

¼ teaspoon crushed red
   pepper
1 teaspoon powdered mustard
½ cup yogurt

Place all ingredients except yogurt in food chopper. Use fine blade or high-speed blender. Grind smooth. Add yogurt. Beat smooth. *Yield* 1½ cups

PEANUT SAUCE
[*Moongphali Thovayal*]

½ cup peanut butter
¼ teaspoon hot-pepper sauce
2 tablespoons tomato purée

⅛ teaspoon salt
1 teaspoon lime juice

Combine all ingredients. Mix well. Serve with chicken livers. *Yield* ½ cup

PICKLED PINEAPPLE
[*Achchar Ananas*]

1 teaspoon freshly ground
   black pepper
¼ teaspoon ground cloves
¼ teaspoon ground cinnamon
½ teaspoon cayenne

1 teaspoon salt
2 cups crushed pineapple,
   drained
1 cup vinegar

Mix together pepper, cloves, cinnamon, cayenne, and salt. Place pineapple on flat dish. Sprinkle pineapple with mixed spices. Set aside for 1 hour. Pour vinegar in saucepan. Heat to warm. Add pineapple. Simmer 3 or 4 minutes. Remove from heat. Cool slowly. *Yield* 4 servings

LIME PICKLE
[*Achchar Nimbu*]

25 *limes, cut in eighths*
½ *cup salt*
2 *teaspoons ground turmeric*
2 *teaspoons cayenne*
½ *cup sliced preserved ginger*

¼ *cup brown sugar*
2 *cups salad oil*
2 *teaspoons mustard seeds*
2 *teaspoons crushed lentils*

Combine limes and salt in bowl. Cover. Mix well. Marinate for 2 days. Sprinkle turmeric and cayenne over limes. Add ginger and sugar. Mix well. Pack in a jar. Heat salad oil in skillet. Add mustard seeds. Fry 3 or 4 minutes. Add crushed lentils. Fry 3 or 4 minutes. Pour seasoned oil into jar over limes. Dig ice pick or skewer into limes to allow oil to permeate. Cover jar. Marinate for at least two weeks. *Yield* 2 quarts

ARAB PICKLE
[*Arab Achchar*]

2½ *cups sugar*
4 *cups vinegar*
1 *tablespoon freshly ground
   black pepper*
1 *tablespoon ground
   cinnamon*

1 *tablespoon ground ginger*
½ *pound dry apricots, diced*
½ *pound dry apples, diced*
½ *pound pitted dates, diced*
½ *pound pitted prunes, diced*

Combine sugar, vinegar, pepper, cinnamon, and ginger in large pan. Cover. Boil 5 minutes. Remove from heat. Add apricots, apples, dates, and prunes. Mix well. Spoon into jars. Cover tightly. Marinate for 2 weeks. *Yield* 2 quarts

PICKLED EGGS
[*Achchar Unday*]

3 cups vinegar
6 garlic cloves, crushed
1 teaspoon ground ginger
1 teaspoon freshly ground
  black pepper

1 teaspoon allspice
2 teaspoons salt
12 hard-boiled eggs

Combine vinegar, garlic, ginger, pepper, allspice, and salt in saucepan. Boil 3 or 4 minutes. Make cuts in eggs. Be careful not to cut too deep. Place eggs in casserole. Pour boiled vinegar and spices over eggs. Cover. Place on medium heat until starting to boil. Remove and allow to cool. *Yield* 6 servings

Note: Mushrooms may be pickled the same way. Add a pinch of sugar to vinegar.

SPICE-STUFFED PEPPERS
[*Masalah Bhara Mircha*]

6 large green bell peppers
4 slivers of garlic
1 teaspoon ground ginger
Whole dry green or red
  pepper, to taste
1 teaspoon coriander leaves
½ teaspoon ground turmeric

Chili powder to taste
Salt to taste
2 tablespoons water
2 medium onions, thinly
  sliced
2 tablespoons lentils, soaked
  for 2 hours

Cut a slit lengthwise in peppers and remove seeds. Be careful not to split peppers. Wash and dry peppers. Blend all the spices in water. Mix onions, lentils, and spices together, spoon into casserole with 1 tablespoon of vegetable shortening that has been heated. Lightly fry for a few minutes and stuff into each pepper. Add 2 tablespoons of vegetable shortening to same heated casserole and place peppers in. Cover casserole and cook on low heat.

Sprinkle with water occasionally. When tender, remove cover and add 1 tablespoon of vegetable shortening and fry on all sides until light brown. *Yield* 3 to 4 servings

SHRIMP PRESERVE
[*Chota Ghinga Ballachung*]

2 *cups shrimp, cleaned*

2 *tablespoons ground ginger*

1 *tablespoon lemon pulp*

2 *teaspoons minced garlic*

2 *teaspoons anchovy paste*

1 *cup vegetable oil*

½ *cup sliced scallion tips*

2 *tablespoons chopped green pepper*

1 *tablespoon lemon juice*

1 *cup vinegar*

Place shrimp, ginger, lemon pulp, garlic, and anchovy paste in food chopper. Use fine blade or high-speed blender. Grind to a paste. Heat vegetable oil in skillet. Add scallions. Fry 2 or 3 minutes, not stirring. Add green pepper. Fry slowly until pepper and scallions are soft. Add shrimp paste. Cover. Simmer until steam comes through cover. Sprinkle in lemon juice. Stir until juice is absorbed. Add vinegar. Simmer uncovered until oil begins to separate. Remove from heat. Cool. Spoon into jar. Cover tightly. Reserve for 1 or 2 days before using. *Yield* 6 to 8 servings

SEASONED TOMATOES AND YOGURT
[*Tamatar Pachadi*]

1 *tablespoon vegetable shortening, melted*

1 *teaspoon mustard seeds*

1 *tomato, diced*

½ *onion, diced*

2 *tablespoons green pepper, minced*

Salt

2 *tablespoons yogurt*

Heat shortening in medium-size saucepan. Add mustard seeds, tomato, onion, green pepper, and salt. Simmer until vegetables are tender. Stir in yogurt. Serve. *Yield* 2 servings

SPICED BANANAS IN YOGURT
[*Plantain Pachadi*]

¼ cup grated coconut	1 teaspoon salt
1 cup yogurt	2 cups sliced ripe bananas
2 teaspoons powdered mustard	1 tablespoon lime juice
¼ teaspoon cayenne	

Place coconut in food chopper. Use fine blade or high-speed blender. Grind to a paste. Place yogurt, mustard, cayenne, salt, and coconut paste in bowl. Beat together until smooth. Place bananas in serving bowl. Sprinkle with lime juice. Arrange bananas and yogurt mixture in layers, topping with yogurt mixture. *Yield* 2 to 4 servings

COLE SLAW
[*Vellarikai Pachadi*]

1 cup shredded coconut	1 cup yogurt
2 dashes of hot-pepper sauce	1 teaspoon vegetable
1 large cucumber, peeled and	shortening
grated	1 teaspoon mustard seeds
Salt to taste	

Grind coconut and hot-pepper sauce together in a food chopper using fine blade so coconut becomes a paste. Add coconut paste, cucumber, and salt to yogurt. Mix well. In a deep round spoon heat shortening and fry mustard seeds until they burst. Pour over *pachadi. Yield* 4 servings

SEASONED YOGURT
[Curd Pachadi]

2 cups yogurt	¼ teaspoon chili sauce
½ cup finely chopped onion	½ teaspoon ground cumin
2 tablespoons chopped parsley or coriander leaves	Salt to taste

Place all ingredients in salad bowl. Mix well. Serve. *Yield* 4 servings

CUCUMBER AND YOGURT
[Kheera Raita]

1 tablespoon vegetable shortening	2 teaspoons ginger
	2 teaspoons sugar
1 teaspoon mustard seeds	Salt
1 onion, chopped	1 cup yogurt
3 teaspoons green pepper, minced	1 cucumber, peeled, finely chopped

Heat shortening until very hot. Add mustard seeds. When seeds begin to crackle, add onion, green pepper, ginger, sugar, and salt. Cook over low heat until onion is soft but not brown. Remove from heat. Stir in yogurt and cucumber. Chill for 1 hour. *Yield* 4 servings

PUMPKIN IN YOGURT
[Kuddoo Raita]

1 cup cooked pumpkin	Salt to taste
¼ cup yogurt	1 tablespoon vegetable shortening
1½-inch piece of ginger, finely sliced	
Whole dry red or green pepper, finely sliced, to taste	¼ teaspoon mustard seeds
	¼ teaspoon cumin seeds

Heat pumpkin in saucepan. When most of moisture is cooked off, add yogurt, ginger, pepper, and salt. In deep round spoon, heat vegetable shortening and fry mustard seeds and cumin seeds and pour over *raita*. Yield 4 servings

EGGPLANT AND YOGURT
[*Brinjal Raita*]

½ onion, chopped
½ tablespoon vegetable
  shortening
1 teaspoon ginger
⅛ teaspoon salt
⅛ teaspoon sugar

1 cup yogurt
⅛ teaspoon dill
½ teaspoon parsley, minced
1 eggplant, peeled, finely
  chopped, and deep fried

Sauté onion in shortening until onion is soft. Add ginger, salt, and sugar. Stir in yogurt. Remove from heat. Add dill, parsley, and eggplant. Serve warm. Yield 4 servings

CUCUMBER AND YOGURT
[*Kheera Raita*]

1 cucumber, peeled
½ teaspoon salt
1½ cups yogurt

Paprika
Ground black pepper

Grate cucumber. Add salt. Let stand for several hours. Drain and squeeze out water. Beat yogurt and fold in cucumber. Garnish with paprika and black pepper. Yield 8 servings

Rice

ORANGE RICE
[Narrangee Chawal]

2 cups orange juice
1 tablespoon butter or
  margarine
1 tablespoon sugar
1 cup rice

2 tablespoons orange-juice
  concentrate
2 tablespoons orange rind,
  grated

Bring orange juice to a boil in medium saucepan. Stir in butter or margarine and sugar. Add rice; stir to mix. Cover. Simmer over low heat until rice is tender and liquid is absorbed, about 20 minutes. Add concentrate and orange rind. *Yield* 4 servings

LIME RICE
[Puli Saatham]

¼ cup vegetable oil
½ cup split chick-peas, soaked
  2 to 3 hours
½ cup lime juice
½ tablespoon ground
  turmeric

1 teaspoon ground ginger
½ teaspoon cayenne pepper
1 teaspoon sugar
Salt to taste
4 cups half-cooked rice

Heat vegetable oil in large skillet and fry chick-peas until crisp. Mix together lime juice, turmeric, ginger, cayenne, sugar, and salt. Pour seasoned lime juice over chick-peas. Allow to become hot, but not boiling. Add rice and mix well. Steam rice until done. *Yield* 4 to 5 servings

SESAME RICE
[*Ell Parimall*]

1 cup small white onions
Salted water
2 tablespoons sesame seeds
4 cups half-cooked rice
¼ cup vegetable shortening
1 teaspoon mustard seeds
1 teaspoon ground black
    pepper

¼ teaspoon cayenne pepper
½ teaspoon ground cumin
1 teaspoon brown sugar
Salt to taste
Rose water, a sprinkling

Cook onions in salted water until half done. Roast sesame seeds in
dry skillet until they stop sputtering. Place rice in steamer and
add sesame seeds, mix well. Add onions to rice. Heat shortening
in skillet and add mustard seeds. Fry for a few minutes. Add black
pepper, cayenne, cumin, brown sugar, and salt. Fry for a few
minutes and pour into rice. Steam rice until done. Sprinkle with
rose water. *Yield* 4 to 6 servings

COCONUT RICE
[*Nariul Chawal*]

4 cups raw rice
1 cup grated coconut
2 tablespoons butter or
    margarine
½ cup chopped bell pepper
2 tablespoons vegetable
    shortening

2 tablespoons chick-peas,
    soaked in water
¼ cup raisins
1 teaspoon mustard seeds
1 teaspoon ground turmeric
2 teaspoons salt
1 teaspoon ground cardamom

Place rice, coconut, and butter or margarine in steamer or pressure
pot with sufficient water to steam. When rice is steamed add
pepper, mix lightly and keep covered. Heat shortening in large
skillet and fry chick-peas until crisp. Add raisins, mustard seeds,
turmeric, salt, and cardamon to chick-peas and fry for a few

minutes. Remove from skillet and add to rice, mixing well. Keep hot and serve. *Yield* 8 to 10 servings

SWEET RICE
[Pongal]

¼ cup sweet butter
2 cups rice
2 teaspoons freshly ground
   black pepper
1 tablespoon ground ginger
½ teaspoon ground cloves

1 cup grated coconut
4 cups milk
1 cup crushed sugar candy
½ teaspoon saffron soaked in
   2 tablespoons milk
2 teaspoons rose water

Melt butter in casserole. Add rice. Fry until hot. Add pepper, ginger, cloves, and coconut. Fry 2 or 3 minutes. Add milk. Cook rice until tender. Add candy. Stir quickly. Reduce heat just enough to keep hot. Sprinkle saffron milk over rice. Serve hot. *Yield* 6 to 8 servings

RICE AND MEATBALL CASSEROLE
[Moti Pulao]

½ pound fine ground beef
½ teaspoon ground coriander
Whole dry red or green
   pepper, chopped to taste
½ teaspoon ground
   cardamom
¼ teaspoon ground cinnamon
¼ teaspoon ground cloves
Salt to taste
1 egg
4 tablespoons vegetable
   shortening, divided
2 medium onions, sliced
   thin

½ teaspoon ground ginger
Sugar to taste
2 bay leaves
Whole dry green or red
   pepper, chopped, to taste
¾ teaspoon ground turmeric
1 teaspoon ground coriander
Chili powder to taste
Salt to taste
3 cups hot cooked rice
1 medium onion, sliced thin
Butter or margarine

In a mixing bowl place ground beef, coriander, pepper, cardamom, cinnamon, cloves, salt, and egg. Mix well and make small balls the size of marbles. Heat 2 tablespoons shortening in skillet and add meatballs. Fry until well browned. Reserve and keep warm. Heat 2 tablespoons of shortening in skillet and brown onions with ginger and sugar. Add bay leaves, pepper, turmeric, coriander, chili powder, and salt. Fry for a few minutes. Add rice and mix. In a casserole arrange alternate layers of rice and meatballs. The last layer should be rice. Cover and dot with butter or margarine and place casserole in 325° oven for 20 minutes. Fry onions crisp and garnish meat and rice. *Yield* 4 servings

SHRIMP AND VEGETABLES WITH RICE
[*Chota Ginga Thurkaree Pulao*]

1 *pound shrimp*	1 *cup cauliflower flowerets*
Salted water	1 *cup carrots, diced*
Pinch of turmeric	½ *cup broccoli, long strips*
½ *cup vegetable shortening*	2 *tablespoons vinegar*
1 *onion, sliced thin*	*Water*
2 *teaspoons turmeric*	1 *cup peas*
1½ *teaspoons cinnamon*	2 *tablespoons green pepper,*
1 *teaspoon cloves*	*chopped*
1 *teaspoon ginger*	1 *tomato, chopped*
1 *teaspoon red pepper*	1 *cup celery, chopped*
2 *teaspoons anise*	½ *cup parsley or coriander*
1 *teaspoon sugar*	*leaves, chopped*
Salt	2 *cups cooked rice*
6 *cloves garlic, sliced thin*	

Marinate shrimp in salted water with a pinch of turmeric for 15 minutes. Drain. Heat ¼ cup of the shortening. Fry shrimp in shortening until tender. Set aside. Add remaining shortening to skillet. Add onion and fry until tender. Add turmeric, cinnamon, cloves, ginger, red pepper, anise, sugar, and salt. Stir to mix. Add garlic, cauliflower, carrots, broccoli, vinegar, and a small amount of water. Cover. Simmer 5 minutes. Add peas, green pepper, and shrimp. Cook 1 minute. Stir in tomato, celery, and parsley. Add to cooked rice; mix. Serve. *Yield* 4 servings

RICE AND CHEESE
[Kashmiri Pulao]

¼ cup milk
2 tablespoons unsalted
   pistachio nuts
2 tablespoons almonds
1 cup cranberries
1 cup raisins
1½ quarts hot beef bouillon,
   divided
¼ cup vegetable shortening
2 cups pot cheese, squeezed
   dry
1 tablespoon ground ginger

1 tablespoon ground
   cardamom
1 tablespoon ground
   coriander
1 teaspoon ground cinnamon
3 cloves
12 anise seeds
2 cups rice
½ cup cooked sliced
   mushrooms
1 tablespoon saffron
2 tablespoons lime juice

Pour milk in saucepan. Boil. Add pistachios and almonds. Boil for 5 minutes. Set aside. Cool. Soak cranberries and raisins in 2 cups of bouillon. Heat vegetable shortening in large skillet. Add pot cheese. Fry until brown. Remove cheese. Add ginger, cardamom, coriander, cinnamon, cloves, and anise seeds. Fry 2 or 3 minutes. Add rice, mushrooms, and remaining bouillon to 1 inch above rice. Cover. Cook until rice is almost done. Add nuts, cranberries, and raisins. Cover. Cook until steam escapes through cover. Sprinkle in fried pot cheese, saffron, and lime juice. Cover. Cook until cranberries and rice are soft. Serve. *Yield* 6 to 8 servings

RICE AND SHRIMP
[*Jheenga Pulao*]

4 tablespoons vegetable
    shortening
2 cups shrimp, cleaned and
    deveined
1 medium onion, thinly sliced
1 large tomato, sliced thick
4 green bell peppers, sliced
    in rings

Salt to taste
3 cups hot cooked rice
½ cup cooked peas
¼ cup cooked diced carrots
1 two-egg omelet, chopped
Butter or margarine
1 medium onion, thinly
    sliced

Heat shortening in skillet and fry shrimp, onion, tomato, and
peppers, until almost dry. Add salt. In a mixing bowl, combine
the rice, peas, carrots, and chopped omelet. Spread the egg-and-
vegetable mixture over the shrimp mixture. Dot with butter or
margarine. Cover and cook slowly for a few minutes until margarine has melted. Crisp fry onion. Garnish *pulao* with onion rings.
Yield 4 servings

RICE AND VEGETABLES
[*Sabzi Pulao*]

2 medium onions
6 slivers of garlic
1 two-inch piece fresh ginger
⅛ teaspoon coriander leaves
⅛ teaspoon mint leaves
4 cardamoms
Whole dry green or red
    pepper to taste
4 cloves
1 one-inch stick cinnamon
1 teaspoon ground turmeric
3 teaspoons poppy seeds
Cayenne or red pepper to
    taste
Salt to taste
3 medium onions, thinly
    sliced

2 tablespoons vegetable
    shortening
2 large tomatoes, quartered
⅔ cup diced carrots
½ cup peas
3 boiled potatoes, sliced
¾ cup cauliflower buds
3 cups cooked rice
Butter or margarine
¼ cup milk
1 teaspoon saffron
10 blanched almonds, sliced
¼ cup raisins
½ teaspoon vegetable
    shortening

Place 2 onions and next 12 ingredients in food chopper using fine blade or high-speed blender and grind together to a paste. Brown sliced onions in vegetable shortening until crisp. Add ground onion and spice paste. Fry for 5 minutes. Add tomatoes, carrots, peas, and cook on low heat until half done. Add potatoes and cauliflower buds and cook until done. In a casserole place half the vegetables and cover with a layer of rice; repeat until all the vegetables and rice are used up. Dot generously with butter or margarine. Heat milk in small pan and add saffron. Let cook for one minute. Sprinkle saffron milk over rice in casserole. Cover casserole and place in 300° oven for 30 minutes. Place almonds and raisins in small skillet and fry in a ½ teaspoon vegetable shortening for a few minutes or until almonds are light brown. Garnish rice and vegetable casserole with almonds and raisins. *Yield* 4 servings

LAMB AND RICE
[*Yakhni Pulao*]

1 *pound lamb, cut in cubes*	3 *tablespoons vegetable*
1 *small onion, quartered*	*shortening*
6 *slivers of garlic*	½ *teaspoon crushed garlic*
1 *one-inch piece ginger, sliced*	½ *teaspoon ground ginger*
Whole dry red or green	2 *teaspoons cumin seeds*
pepper, cut to taste	1 *two-inch cinnamon stick*
1 *one-inch stick of cinnamon*	6 *cardamoms*
6 *cloves*	8 *cloves*
2 *teaspoons coriander seeds*	*Salt to taste*
Salt to taste	1 *cup yogurt*
4 *cups water*	1 *cup rice*
1 *large onion, thinly sliced*	3 *hard-boiled eggs, sliced*

Place lamb in pan. Tie in a piece of gauze or muslin bag, the onion, garlic, ginger, pepper, cinnamon, cloves, and coriander seeds. Add salt and water. Slowly bring to a boil. Simmer slowly until lamb is done, approximately 1 hour. Remove bag. In a large skillet or casserole fry onions brown in vegetable shortening and then remove half for garnishing. Add garlic, ginger, cumin seeds, cinnamon, cardamons, cloves, and salt. Fry for 1 minute. Add cooked lamb and yogurt. Fry until meat is browned. Add rice and fry for 5 minutes, if necessary add a small amount of vegetable shortening. Add 2 cups of stock that lamb was cooked in. Cover and cook slowly until rice is cooked. Garnish with reserved browned onions and sliced eggs. *Yield* 4 servings

RICE AND PEANUTS
[*Ghhanar Pulao*]

3 *tablespoons vegetable oil*
½ *cup unsalted peanuts*
2 *bay leaves*
4 *cloves*
1 *two-inch cinnamon stick*
2 *cardamoms*
1 *cup rice*

¼ *cup peas*
Whole dry green or red
  pepper to taste
Salt to taste
Sugar to taste
2 *cups water*
2 *teaspoons raisins*

Heat vegetable oil in skillet and fry peanuts until a golden brown. Set peanuts aside and in same pan add a little more oil and fry bay leaves, cloves, cinnamon, and cardamoms. Add rice and fry for 5 minutes. Add peas, pepper, salt, sugar, and water to cook rice, approximately 20 to 30 minutes. When water is almost absorbed, add peanuts and raisins. Cook slowly until water is completely absorbed and rice is tender. Serve with yogurt. *Yield* 4 servings

RICE STEAMED WITH LAMB
[*Yakhni Pilau*]

2 *pounds lamb shanks*
½ *cup yogurt*
4 *cups cold water*
2½ *teaspoons salt*
2 *cups long-grained rice*
2 *tablespoons vegetable*
  shortening
4 *whole cardamom seeds,*
  cracked

6 *whole cloves*
1 *stick cinnamon, 2 inches*
  long
¼ *teaspoon caraway seeds*
1 *bay leaf*
4 *cups lamb broth and water*
4-*ounce can white mushrooms*

Purchase lean lamb shanks and trim off all excess fat. Mix with yogurt and marinate ½ hour. Add 2 cups of the cold water and 1 teaspoon of the salt. Cover and simmer 3 hours. Cool and trim all lean meat from bones. Discard bones. Save meat to use later. Chill stock. Lift off all the hardened fat and discard it. Set stock aside. Soak rice 30 minutes in remaining 2 cups cold water. Drain well. Melt shortening in a 4-quart saucepan. Tie cardamom seeds and cloves in a cheesecloth bag and add to shortening, along with cinnamon, caraway seeds, and bay leaf. Sauté 2 minutes. Add well-drained rice. Stir and cook 3 to 4 minutes. Add lamb broth and water, remaining salt, meat trimmed from bones, and mushrooms. Cover, and bring to boiling point and boil 15 minutes or until rice is tender and grains stand apart. Do not stir. Lift out spice bag, cinnamon, and bay leaf. Serve hot. *Yield* 8 to 10 servings

CHICKEN AND RICE
[*Biryani*]

1 broiler-fryer chicken, 2½ to 3 pounds
2 medium onions, quartered
6 garlic cloves
1 tablespoon ground ginger
⅛ teaspoon coriander leaves
⅛ teaspoon mint leaves
4 whole cardamoms
⅛ teaspoon ground mace
Whole dry green or red pepper, to taste
4 cloves
2 teaspoons poppy seeds
½ teaspoon ground cinnamon
Salt to taste
2 cups yogurt
1 cup vegetable shortening
3 medium onions, thinly sliced
3½ cups half-cooked rice
Butter or margarine
1 teaspoon saffron
¼ cup warm milk
10 blanched almonds, sliced
2 tablespoons raisins
4 hard-boiled eggs, sliced

Cut chicken into 12 or 14 pieces. Grind to paste in food chopper using fine blade or high-speed blender: quartered onions, garlic, ginger, coriander, mint, cardamoms, mace, pepper, cloves, poppy seeds, cinnamon, and salt. Place chicken in large bowl, add yogurt and spices. Let stand for at least 2 hours. Melt vegetable shortening in large skillet, when hot add sliced onions and fry until crisp. Add onions to the chicken mixture and mix well. Place in large casserole and cook on low heat until chicken is almost tender, approximately 1 hour. Remove half of chicken and cover chicken in casserole with layer of rice. Repeat until chicken and rice are used up. Dot generously with butter or margarine. Heat and crush saffron in milk. Sprinkle saffron milk over rice and chicken. Cover and seal casserole tightly. A good way to seal is to use a dough around the edges. Allow to steam over low heat for ½ hour. Before serving, fry almonds and raisins in a little shortening until almonds are golden brown. Garnish chicken with eggs, almonds, and raisins. *Yield* 4 servings

MADRAS CHICKEN PILAU
[Neye Saatham]

5-pound fricassee chicken
3 cups cold water
½ cup chopped onion
3 teaspoons salt, divided
6 peppercorns
1 cup rice
2 cups water

2 tablespoons butter or
 margarine
3 teaspoons curry powder
2 cups chicken stock
¼ cup seedless raisins
¼ cup slivered, blanched,
 toasted almonds

Wash chicken and cut into serving-size pieces. Place in a 2-quart saucepan with water, onion, 2 teaspoons of the salt, and peppercorns. Cover and cook slowly 1 hour or until chicken is tender. Soak rice in the 2 cups water for 30 minutes. Drain. Stir and cook in butter or margarine along with curry powder 2 to 3 minutes or until rice sticks to the pan. Add chicken stock and the remaining 1 teaspoon of the salt. Cover and cook 15 minutes or until rice is tender and all water is absorbed. Carefully stir in raisins and almonds. To serve, place a layer of rice on a serving dish on which place the cooked chicken. Cover with remaining rice. *Yield* 6 servings

RICE IN TOMATO JUICE
[Tomato Bhat]

4 tablespoons vegetable
 shortening
1 large onion, thinly sliced
1 garlic clove, crushed
1¼ teaspoons ground ginger

1 peppercorn
3 cloves
1 cup raw rice
2 cups tomato juice
Salt to taste

Heat vegetable shortening in large skillet. Fry onion until brown. Remove half for garnishing. Combine garlic and ginger. Mash together. Add to skillet. Add peppercorns and cloves to skillet.

Fry for 5 minutes. Add rice and fry 2 or 3 minutes. Add tomato juice to cover rice. Add salt. Cook until rice is tender, approximately ½ hour. Garnish with browned onions. *Yield* 4 servings

RICE AND EGGPLANT
[*Ravaiya Bhat*]

6 *tablespoons vegetable shortening, divided*
½ *teaspoon ground cumin*
1½ *teaspoons ground coriander*
1 *teaspoon ground turmeric*
Chili powder to taste
Salt to taste

Sugar to taste
1 *tablespoon lime juice*
1 *teaspoon lentil flour*
1 *large potato, 4 slices lengthwise*
4 *slices eggplant*
3 *cups cooked rice*
Butter or margarine

Heat 1 tablespoon vegetable shortening in small skillet. Add, separately, cumin, coriander, turmeric, chili powder, salt, sugar, lime juice, and lentil flour, stirring as each ingredient is added. Heat 5 tablespoons vegetable shortening. Add potatoes, and eggplant. Mash ½ of fried spices on top of potatoes and eggplant. Fry 2 or 3 minutes. Turn over and add remainder of spices on top of potatoes and eggplant. Fry slowly for 5 minutes. Add a little water to allow vegetables to cook until done. Cover with layer of rice. Dot with butter or margarine. Cover and steam for 10 minutes. *Yield* 4 servings

RICE AND EGGPLANT
[*Wangi Bhat*]

Crushed red pepper to taste
¾ teaspoon ground mustard seeds
¾ teaspoon ground cumin seeds
1 teaspoon poppy seeds
3 slivers of garlic
½ teaspoon ground turmeric
¼ teaspoon freshly ground pepper
¼ teaspoon ground cloves
1 teaspoon ground cinnamon
2 tablespoons crushed peanuts
Salt to taste
1 pound eggplant, sliced thick
8 tablespoons vegetable shortening, divided
1 large onion, thinly sliced
3 cups hot cooked rice
½ coconut, grated

Place crushed red pepper, mustard, cumin, poppy seeds, garlic, turmeric, pepper, cloves, cinnamon, peanuts, and salt in a small bowl with enough water to make a paste. Rub eggplant slices with spice paste. Set aside. Heat 6 tablespoons vegetable shortening and fry onion light brown. Add eggplant, fry approximately 20 minutes or until done. Sprinkle with water if necessary. Heat remaining vegetable shortening in a separate skillet. Add rice. Fry 4 or 5 minutes. Salt and cover. In a serving dish arrange eggplant and rice in layers. Garnish with coconut. Serve hot. *Yield* 4 servings

RICE AND CABBAGE
[*Cobi Bhat*]

1 cup rice
⅛ teaspoon garlic powder
1 whole ginger—1-inch long
¼ teaspoon ground red
   pepper
¼ teaspoon mustard seeds
½ teaspoon cumin seeds
1 teaspoon poppy seeds

1 stick cinnamon—½-inch
   long
Salt to taste
5 tablespoons vegetable
   shortening
1 large onion, finely chopped
¼ pound cabbage, finely
   chopped
1½ cups shredded coconut

Wash and soak rice for ½ hour. While rice is soaking, place all spices in food chopper using the finest blade. Grind spice finely. If necessary place through chopper twice. Heat shortening in pan and sauté onions. Add rice, finely ground spices and cabbage. Fry for a few minutes. Add water to cover and cook until rice is tender, approximately ½ hour. Garnish with coconut. *Yield* 4 servings

RICE, BEANS, AND RAISINS
[*Leelvani Khichadi*]

5 tablespoons vegetable
   shortening
8 cloves
½ cup raisins
1 cup raw rice

½ pound string beans, cut in
   long slices
1¼ teaspoons ground ginger
2 almonds, crushed
1 teaspoon crushed peanuts
Salt to taste

Heat vegetable shortening in large skillet. Add cloves and raisins. Fry for 1 minute. Add rice and beans. Fry until rice begins to stick to bottom of skillet. Add water to cover ½ inch above rice level. Add remaining ingredients, cover tightly and simmer until rice and beans are tender, approximately ½ hour. Serve. *Yield* 4 servings

RICE AND PEAS
[*Masala Khichadi*]

5 tablespoons vegetable
    shortening
1 large onion, thinly sliced
1 garlic clove, crushed
1¼ teaspoons ground ginger

Salt to taste
1 cup raw rice
½ cup peas
1 teaspoon ground cinnamon
4 cloves

Heat shortening in large skillet. Fry onions until brown. Combine garlic and ginger in small bowl. Remove half of fried onions from skillet for garnishing. Add ginger and garlic paste and salt to skillet. Fry until brown. Add rice and peas. Fry for 3 or 4 minutes. Add water to cover, cinnamon, and cloves. Simmer until rice and peas are tender, approximately ½ hour. Garnish with reserved browned onions. *Yield* 4 servings

RICE PILAF
[*Lall Chaaval*]

2 tablespoons vegetable
    shortening
1 medium onion, sliced
1 tablespoon cumin seeds
½ teaspoon ground
    cardamom
⅛ teaspoon ground cloves

1 bay leaf
2 teaspoons brown sugar
1 tablespoon salt
2¼ cups rice, washed and
    drained
4 cups boiling water

Heat vegetable shortening in large skillet. Add onion. Fry 1 or 2 minutes. Add cumin seeds, cardamom, cloves, bay leaf, sugar, and salt. Fry slowly until onion is browned. Add rice. Fry slowly until rice is dry. Pour in boiling water to 2 inches above rice. Cover. Cook slowly until rice is tender, approximately ½ hour. *Yield* 4 to 6 servings

TANJORE BEANS WITH RICE
[*Tanjore Kaai-Saatham*]

½ cup sweet butter	1 cup raw rice
1 teaspoon mustard seeds	Salt to taste
½ teaspoon ground ginger	1 cup raisins
2 cups 1-inch pieces snap beans	2 tablespoons chopped nuts
4 cloves, crushed	Part water and part white wine for cooking

Heat butter in large skillet. Add mustard seeds and fry for few minutes. Add ginger and fry for few minutes. Add beans and fry for 2 to 3 minutes. Sprinkle in cloves. Add rice and salt. Cover with just enough water to cook rice. Cook slowly. Add raisins when rice is cooked, approximately ½ hour. Cover and allow raisins to soften. Sprinkle with nuts before serving. *Yield* 4 to 5 servings

RICE AND SPLIT PEAS
[*Daal Khichadi*]

1 cup raw rice	4 whole cardamoms, crushed
1 cup lentils or split peas	4 cloves, crushed
¼ cup vegetable shortening	¼ teaspoon ground black pepper
2 medium onions, thinly sliced	Hot water
1 one-inch cinnamon stick	

Wash rice and lentils separately. Steep in warm water for half an hour. Heat shortening in large skillet and fry onions until crisp. Remove and keep warm. Drain lentils. Fry until water is evaporated. Drain rice and add to frying lentils. Add cinnamon, cardamoms, cloves, and black pepper. Stir well. Pour on hot water to reach 2 inches above level of rice. Cover tightly. Cook over slow heat until rice is cooked, approximately ½ hour. Place rice in serving dish and cover with crisp onions. Serve with yogurt. *Yield* 4 to 6 servings

FRIED PUFFED RICE
[*Churmure*]

2 cups puffed cereal rice
3 tablespoons vegetable
  shortening
½ cup chopped parsley
  or coriander leaves
½ cup chopped coconut

½ cup crushed cashew nuts
½ cup raisins
1 teaspoon ground turmeric
1 teaspoon cayenne
2 teaspoons salt
1 teaspoon sugar

Dampen puffed rice in water. Drain in colander. Rice must be separate, but not soggy. Heat vegetable shortening in large skillet. Add each ingredient in order. Fry for one minute each, parsley, coconut, cashew nuts, raisins, turmeric, cayenne, salt, sugar, and puffed rice. Stir after each ingredient is added. Fry entire mixture until puffed rice is dry. *Yield* 6 to 8 servings

RICE AND YOGURT
[*Thayir Saatham*]

2 cups yogurt
½ teaspoon ground ginger
Salt to taste
4 cups cooked rice
¼ cup vegetable shortening
¼ teaspoon crushed red
  pepper

1 teaspoon chick-peas, soaked
  2 hours
1 teaspoon split peas, soaked
  2 hours
1 teaspoon mustard seeds
Cashew nuts

Combine yogurt, ginger and salt. Beat smooth. Stir into rice. Heat vegetable shortening in large skillet. Add crushed red pepper and fry for a few minutes. Add chick-peas, split peas, and mustard seeds. Fry until peas are soft, approximately ½ hour. Pour fried peas and spices into rice. Stir lightly. Serve cold, sprinkled with cashew nuts. *Yield* 6 servings

LEFT-OVER RICE
[*Ell Shadham*]

1 *tablespoon vegetable shortening*	2 *cups cooked rice*
1 *teaspoon lentils, soaked*	2 *tablespoons ground roasted sesame seeds*
1 *teaspoon ground mustard seeds*	*Crushed red pepper to taste*
⅛ *teaspoon curry powder*	*Salt to taste*

Heat vegetable shortening in small skillet. Add lentils, mustard seeds, and curry powder. Fry 2 to 3 minutes. Heat rice in double boiler. Place rice in serving bowl. Pour over fried spices. Add sesame seeds, crushed red pepper, and salt. Mix well. *Yield* 4 servings

RICE SALAD
[*Butty*]

3½ *cups cool cooked rice*	*Crushed red peppers to taste*
½ *cup yogurt*	½ *medium onion, diced*
½ *garlic clove, crushed*	¼ *cup milk*
1 *teaspoon ground coriander*	*Salt to taste*

Place rice in serving bowl. Add all ingredients. Mix well. Serve cold. *Yield* 4 servings

FRIED RICE CAKES
[Atharse]

1 cup rice, soaked overnight, drain and dry slightly

2 tablespoons butter or margarine

1 cup boiling molasses

4 tablespoons thickly cooked farina

1 tablespoon rice flour

2 tablespoons water

1 tablespoon poppy seeds

1 teaspoon ground ginger

1 teaspoon ground anise

Vegetable shortening for deep frying

Place rice in food chopper. Use fine blade or high-speed blender. Grind finely. Place rice in mixing bowl. Rub butter or margarine in rice. Add molasses. Mix well. Combine farina, rice flour, and water. Add to batter. Mix well. Set aside for 2 days. Divide into 14 small balls. Smear board with vegetable shortening. Sprinkle poppy seeds, ginger, and anise on board. Flatten balls on board. Flatten each ball about 2 inches in diameter. Heat vegetable shortening for deep frying in skillet. Fry rice cakes until brown. Yield 14 atharse

TIFFIN

In some regions of India the cold weather is mild and summer mornings break very early. The meals are arranged as follows:

Coffee	5:30 A.M.
Brunch	10:30 A.M.
High Tea or	
Tiffin	3:30 P.M.
Supper	7:30 P.M.

Coffee will be ready in the decantation maker for those who want it before bed. Even offices open and shut to coincide with these timings. For tiffin, two or three tidbits are eaten, only one of which may be freshly made. The literal translation of the Tamil word for tiffin means "Many tastes."

Tiffin:
Sweet Snacks and
Savories

SWEET-BUTTER CAKES
[Makhan Vada]

2¼ cups flour
½ cup sweet butter
3 tablespoons yogurt

1¼ cups sugar
⅔ cup water
¼ cup vegetable shortening

Combine flour and ½ cup butter in mixing bowl. Blend well.
Add 3 tablespoons of yogurt. Knead to soft dough. Add a little
more yogurt if necessary. Divide into 24 small rounded discs.
Combine sugar and water in saucepan. Cover. Boil 5 minutes.
Remove from heat. Heat ¼ cup vegetable shortening in skillet.
Fry rounded discs until light brown. Drain. Soak in syrup. Re-
move. Yield 24 pieces

BANANA CAKES
[Paniyaram]

1 cup rice flour
½ cup farina
1 cup brown sugar
1 cup mashed ripe bananas

1 teaspoon ground fennel
1 teaspoon bicarbonate of
soda
Thick coconut milk

Combine flour, farina, and brown sugar in mixing bowl. Knead
to a thick dough, adding as little water as necessary. Reserve in
warm place overnight. Add bananas, fennel, and bicarbonate of

soda. Add enough coconut milk to thin out to pancake-batter consistency. Beat well. Heat griddle. Smear with butter. Pour batter on griddle as for pancakes. *Yield* 1½ to 2 dozen

COCONUT ROLLS
[*Patishapta*]

½ cup dry powdered milk
¼ cup cream
1 tablespoon vegetable
  shortening
2 cups grated coconut
½ teaspoon ground
  cardamom

2 tablespoons sugar
1 cup flour
⅛ teaspoon salt
1 cup milk
3 tablespoons vegetable
  shortening

Blend together powdered milk and cream. Rub to a smooth paste. Heat 1 tablespoon vegetable shortening in skillet. Add coconut, cardamom, and sugar. Stir and fry until golden brown. Remove from heat. Add powdered milk and cream paste. Mix well. Cool. Sift together flour and salt. Add milk. Beat until smooth. Heat 3 tablespoons of vegetable shortening in skillet. Pour in 2 tablespoons of the batter and allow to spread thinly. Fry for 1 minute. Turn and fry again for 1 minute. Remove from skillet. Place 1 tablespoon of coconut mixture in the center and roll. *Yield* 10 pieces

SWEET FRIED CAKES
[*Shankar Pale*]

1 tablespoon butter or
  margarine
1 cup whole-wheat flour

½ cup powdered sugar
Vegetable shortening for
  deep frying

Rub butter or margarine into flour. Add powdered sugar. Add just enough water to knead to a soft dough. Roll out into large thick *chapati*. Cut into small diamonds. Heat vegetable shortening for deep frying in skillet. Deep-fry until light brown. *Yield* 18 pieces

FRIED CAKES
[*Chirote*]

1 cup flour
1 tablespoon sweet butter or
   margarine

Vegetable shortening for
   deep frying
1 cup powdered sugar

Place flour in mixing bowl. Rub 1 tablespoon butter or margarine
in flour. Knead to a soft dough. Divide into 12 balls. Roll out
each ball into a thin round about 6-inch diameter. Take one
round, smear with a little butter or margarine. Sprinkle with flour.
Place another round on top. Repeat until all rounds are used.
Smear top round with butter or margarine. Roll out the stacked
rounds. Cut into ½-inch pieces. Flatten each piece with cut side
up. Roll in oblong shape. Fry until light brown. Remove. Drain
on absorbent paper. Sprinkle with sugar. *Yield* 14 pieces

COCONUT COOKIES
[*Nan Khatai*]

2¼ cups sifted all-purpose
   flour
1½ teaspoons double-action
   baking powder
½ teaspoon ground
   cardamom seed
½ teaspoon salt

1¼ cups sugar
1 cup vegetable shortening
2 eggs
Granulated sugar
Desiccated coconut or grated
   fresh coconut

Sift together flour, baking powder, cardamom, and salt. Set aside
to use later. Gradually blend sugar with vegetable shortening. Beat
in eggs. Gradually stir in flour mixture. Drop ½ rounded teaspoon
dough at a time on ungreased cooky sheets. Flatten to ⅛-inch
thickness with a glass covered with a damp cloth. Sprinkle tops
with granulated sugar and coconut. Bake in a preheated moderate
oven (375°) 8 to 10 minutes or until cookies are lightly browned

around the edges. Cool on pans about ½ minute. Remove to wire cooling rack to finish cooling. Store in tightly closed tin boxes or jars. *Yield* about 8 dozen

STEAMED COCONUT CAKES
[*Modak*]

1 *cup brown sugar*	4 *cups rice flour*
½ *cup grated coconut*	4 *teaspoons sweet butter or*
¼ *cup sesame seeds*	*margarine*
1 *tablespoon ground*	4 *cups boiling water*
cardamom	

Place sugar and coconut in saucepan. Heat, stirring until blended together and sticky. Add sesame seeds and cardamom. Mix well. Reserve. Place flour in large bowl. Rub in butter or margarine. Hollow out center of flour. Add water. Mix quickly to make a stiff dough. Sprinkle with more water if too stiff. Mix again. Grease palms of hands. Pinch off a lemon size of dough. Pat into a thick cake, 2 inches in diameter. Make a hole in center of cake with thumb. Fill with coconut mixture. Close up hole. Form into a semicircle. Firmly close down fist on top of dough in order to leave the imprint of four fingers. Wrap each cake in floured cheesecloth. Place on a perforated lid. Steam for 20 minutes. *Yield* 10 to 12 servings

DEEP-FRIED SWEET CAKES
[*Kangan*]

⅓ *cup sugar*	2 *teaspoons baking powder*
2 *tablespoons sweet butter*	¼ *teaspoon salt*
or margarine	8 *blanched almonds, grated*
2 *eggs, beaten*	*Vegetable shortening for*
⅓ *cup milk*	*deep frying*
2 *cups sifted flour*	

Cream together sugar and butter or margarine in large bowl. Add eggs and milk. Mix well. Sift flour, baking powder, and salt together. Add creamed sugar. Mix well. Add almonds. Turn out on lightly floured board. Roll to ½-inch thickness. Cut into rounds about 3 inches in diameter. Cut the center of each round again in 2-inch diameter. Remove center. Heat vegetable shortening for deep frying in skillet. Deep-fry rounds until light brown. Drain on absorbent paper. *Yield* 20 pieces

COCONUT AND FRUIT CAKES
[*Karanji*]

1½ cups grated coconut
¼ cup sugar
¼ cup raisins
¼ cup finely sliced blanched
  almonds
1 teaspoon ground cardamom
1 cup flour

1/16 teaspoon salt
¼ cup farina
1 tablespoon butter or
  margarine
Vegetable shortening for
  deep frying

Place coconut, sugar, raisins, almonds, and cardamom in saucepan. Heat slowly and mix until moisture from coconut is dried up. Reserve. Combine 1 cup flour, salt, and farina in mixing bowl. Rub in 1 tablespoon vegetable shortening. Knead to a soft dough. Divide dough in two. Roll out thick. Smear with butter or margarine. Sprinkle with flour. Combine two thicknesses of dough. Roll out like a thick pancake. Cut in 1-inch pieces. Roll out very thin. Fill with coconut mixture and fold. Seal edges. Heat vegetable shortening for deep frying in skillet. Deep-fry *karanji* until light brown. Remove and drain. *Yield* 14 *karanji*

SWEET YOGURT
[Shreekhand]

2 cups yogurt, water removed   1 tablespoon warm milk
2½ cups confectioners' sugar   1¼ teaspoons ground
1 teaspoon saffron   cardamom

Place yogurt and sugar in bowl. Mix well. Soak saffron in milk.
Add to yogurt and sugar. Add cardamom. Serve with *pooris*.
Yield 4 servings.

SWEET STUFFED CHAPATI
[Pooran Poli]

1 cup lentils   ½ teaspoon ground ginger
¼ teaspoon turmeric   Poori dough at the rate of
1 coconut, grated   1 cup flour for every 4 balls
1⅓ cups molasses   of filling (see index)
1 teaspoon ground cardamom   Butter

Cook lentils, adding turmeric until tender. Place cooked lentils
and coconut in food chopper and grind to a paste. Place molasses
in pan. Add paste. Mix well and cook over low heat, until dry.
Add cardamom and ginger. Shape into small balls the size of
marbles with greased fingers. Set aside. Make *poori* dough using
food chopper. Grease hands. Pinch off dough about equal in
amount to filling. Flatten over the left palm. Place filling ball on
flat dough. Pull dough all over filling and seal entirely, covering
filling. Place on a square of greased paper. Roll out thin to make
a disc. Place on hot greased griddle, paper-side up. When one side
is cooked, paper can be easily peeled off. Turn. Add a little butter
on cooked surface. Stack one on top of another, buttering between
each layer. Yield 2 dozen

CHEESE PANCAKES
[*Chhanar Malpua*]

½ cup unsalted farmer
   cheese
1 tablespoon flour
1/16 teaspoon salt
½ cup milk

1 cup sugar
½ cup water
4 tablespoons vegetable
   shortening

Place cheese in mixing bowl. Rub cheese to a smooth paste. Add flour and salt. Mix well. Add milk. Mix batter to a pouring consistency. Combine sugar and water in saucepan. Cover. Boil for 5 minutes. Remove and reserve. Heat vegetable shortening in skillet. Place 1 tablespoon of batter in hot vegetable shortening. Fry until golden brown. Turn over and fry other side. Remove and drain. Dip into sugar syrup. Serve hot. *Yield* 8 cakes

NUT-AND-RAISIN PUDDING
[*Kesari*]

¼ cup sweet butter
¼ cup chopped unsalted
   cashew nuts
¼ cup raisins
2 cups farina
3 cups milk

½ cup sugar
1 teaspoon ground cardamom
1 teaspoon saffron, soaked
   in 2 tablespoons warm
   milk

Heat butter in skillet. Add cashew nuts and raisins. Fry 3 or 4 minutes. Pour off excess butter and reserve. Shake in farina. Fry until farina begins to brown. Pour milk in saucepan. Boil. Add sugar and cardamom. Add sugar milk to farina when sugar has dissolved. Cover. Simmer until milk is completely absorbed, and farina is dry. Sprinkle saffron over farina. Add reserved butter. Stir lightly with fork. *Yield* 4 servings

CASHEW-NUT SNACKS
[*Kaju Dosai*]

4 cups unsalted cashew nuts
½ cup yogurt
2 cups farina
1 cup thick coconut milk
Water
½ tablespoon ground black
  pepper

1 tablespoon onion powder
¼ cup chopped parsley
  or coriander leaves
Salt to taste
¼ tablespoon baking soda
Butter
Vegetable shortening

Place cashew nuts in yogurt. Soak for 1 hour. Grind to a paste in food chopper. Use fine blade or high-speed blender. Place farina in large bowl. Add nut paste. Thin into batter with coconut milk and sufficient water to make a very thin batter. Add pepper, onion powder, parsley, salt, and baking soda. Stir well. Heat griddle. Grease with ½ butter and ½ vegetable shortening. Pour batter on as for pancakes about 4 inches in diameter. *Yield* 6 to 8 servings

Note: Meat or vegetable may be used for stuffing; fold.

SPICE CAKES
[*Anarse*]

1 cup powdered sugar
1 cup vegetable shortening
1 teaspoon vanilla extract
½ teaspoon ground ginger

1 teaspoon ground nutmeg
½ cup lentil flour
1 teaspoon baking soda
2½ cups all-purpose flour

Cream together sugar and shortening until very light. Beat in vanilla, ginger and nutmeg. Beat in lentil flour and baking soda. Add all-purpose flour and blend well. Grease baking pan. Form dough into walnut-size balls. Press down on top and bottom with thumb and index finger. Place on baking pan, far apart. Bake in 350° F. oven until cakes are bloated convex, hiding the finger depression and slightly browned. *Yield* 5 dozen

Tiffin:
Salt Snacks and
Savories

VEGETABLE FRITTERS
[Thurkaree Pakora]

½ cup chopped spinach
½ cup chopped turnip greens
½ cup chopped onion
1 cup diced pumpkin
¼ cup chili sauce

½ teaspoon salt
1 teaspoon whole thyme
1 cup chick-pea flour
Vegetable shortening for
   deep frying

Mix together spinach, greens, onion, pumpkin, chili sauce, salt, and thyme in mixing bowl. Turn onto large pan or tray. Spread out. Sprinkle flour over vegetables to coat evenly. Sprinkle over a little water to stick flour to vegetables. Heat vegetable shortening for deep frying in skillet. Pinch off a bite size at a time of vegetables. Deep-fry until surface is crisp. *Yield* 4 servings

SHRIMP FRITTERS
[Chota Ginga Pakora]

1 cup small shrimp, cleaned
½ cup grated potatoes
½ cup chopped onion
½ cup chopped parsley
1 tablespoon lime juice

2 tablespoons chili sauce
½ teaspoon salt
Rice flour
Vegetable shortening for
   deep frying

Mix together shrimp, potatoes, onion, parsley, lime juice, chili sauce, and salt in mixing bowl. Turn onto large pan or tray. Sprinkle with just enough rice flour to coat evenly. Heat vegetable shortening for deep frying in skillet. Wet hands. Pinch off a small amount of shrimp mixture at a time. Deep-fry until surface is crisp. *Yield* 4 servings

CHEESE FRITTERS
[*Vilayati Paneer Pakora*]

½ *cup rice flour*   1 *teaspoon salt*
½ *cup chick-pea flour*   ¼ *cup tomato purée or*
1 *cup boiling water*   *yogurt*
1 *cup grated cheese*   1 *cup chopped chives*
1 *teaspoon cayenne*

Place rice flour and chick-pea flour in mixing bowl. Add water, stirring quickly to a paste. Combine cheese, cayenne, salt, tomato purée, and chives in another mixing bowl. Add to paste. Beat well. Form into small marble-size balls. Heat vegetable shortening for deep frying in skillet. Deep-fry balls until brown. Remove and drain. *Yield* 4 to 6 servings

FRITTERS
[*Pakora*]

1 *cup chick-pea flour*   *Vegetable shortening for deep*
⅛ *teaspoon baking powder*   *frying*
Chili powder to taste   1 *small cauliflower, separated*
½ *teaspoon ground*   *in flowerets*
  coriander   1 *small eggplant, sliced thin*
¼ *teaspoon ground turmeric* 8 *spinach leaves*
Salt to taste

Place chick-pea flour and baking powder in mixing bowl. Add enough water to make a thick batter. Beat well. Add chili powder, coriander, turmeric, and salt. Beat well. Heat vegetable shortening for deep frying in large skillet. Dip vegetables in batter. Deep-fry golden brown and crisp. Serve immediately. *Yield* 4 to 6 servings

FARINA CAKES
[*Soojee Vadai*]

2 cups farina
2 cups boiling water
1 cup crushed unsalted
  cashew nuts
1 tablespoon sugar
2 teaspoons pepper

Salt to taste
½ *teaspoon cayenne*
¾ *teaspoon ginger*
1 *cup yogurt*
Vegetable shortening for
  deep frying

Place farina in mixing bowl. Pour boiling water over farina. Add cashew nuts, sugar, pepper, salt, cayenne, and ginger. Knead to a stiff dough adding small amounts of yogurt as needed. Shape into doughnuts. Heat vegetable shortening for deep frying. Deep-fry *vadai* until brown. *Yield* 2 to 2½ dozen

TAPIOCA AND NUT CAKES
[*Sagoo Vadai*]

¼ pound pearl tapioca, soak
  1 hour and drain
1 cup hot mashed potatoes
½ cup crushed peanuts
½ coconut, grated
½ teaspoon ground
  coriander

¼ *teaspoon crushed red*
  peppers
¼ *teaspoon salt*
Vegetable shortening for
  deep frying

Combine all ingredients except shortening. Mix well. Divide into 24 small balls. Flatten. Heat vegetable shortening for deep frying in skillet. Deep-fry *vadai* until golden brown. *Yield* 24 *vadai*

LENTIL SNACKS
[*Aama Vadai*]

1 cup chick-peas
1 cup split peas
1 cup lentils
¼ teaspoon crushed red
   peppers
¼ teaspoon salt
1 teaspoon ground turmeric

2 teaspoons ground cumin
2 teaspoons fresh ground
   pepper
½ cup coconut chips
Vegetable shortening for
   deep frying

Soak chick-peas, split peas, and lentils in warm water for 24 hours.
Place soaked peas, lentils, crushed red peppers, and salt in food
chopper. Use fine blade or high-speed blender. Grind but not to a
paste. Turn into mixing bowl. Add turmeric, cumin, pepper, and
coconut. Mix well. On a buttered paper, form mixture into small
doughnuts. Heat vegetable shortening for deep frying in skillet.
Place *vadai* in hot shortening. Deep-fry until brown. Drain. Yield
1½ to 2 dozen

CORN SNACKS
[*Makai Vadai*]

1 cup chick-peas
4 cups whole-kernel corn
Salt to taste
½ cup chopped parsley
1¼ teaspoons ground ginger

1 teaspoon lime juice
½ cup chopped onion
½ teaspoon cayenne
Vegetable shortening for
   deep frying

Soak chick-peas in warm water for 24 hours. Place soaked chick-
peas and corn in food chopper. Use coarse blade. Grind through
once into mixing bowl. Add salt, parsley, ginger, lime juice, onion,
and cayenne. Mix well. On a buttered paper form mixture into
small donuts. Heat vegetable shortening for deep frying in
skillet. Place *vadai* in hot shortening. Deep-fry until brown.
Drain. Yield 2 to 3 dozen

COLD LENTIL CAKES
[*Dahi Vadai*]

2 cups soaked lentils
2 cups yogurt
½ cup grated coconut
2 tablespoons chopped parsley
  or coriander leaves
Salt to taste
1 teaspoon vegetable
  shortening

2 teaspoons mustard seeds
4 teaspoons lentils
2 garlic cloves
2 teaspoons ground cumin
Pepper to taste
Vegetable shortening for
  deep frying

Soak lentils in warm water for 2 hours. Combine yogurt, coconut, parsley, and salt in shallow dish. Heat 1 teaspoon of vegetable shortening in large round spoon. Add mustard seeds and 4 teaspoons lentils. Fry until mustard seeds stop sputtering. Add to yogurt. Mix well. Place soaked lentils, garlic, and cumin in food chopper. Use fine blade or high-speed blender. Grind smooth. Add salt and pepper to taste. Mix well. On a buttered paper, form mixture into small donuts. Heat vegetable shortening for deep frying in skillet. Place *vadai* in hot shortening. Deep-fry until brown. Drain. Place in yogurt and turn until well soaked. May be eaten cold. *Yield 1½ to 2 dozen*

POTATO CAKES
[*Batata Vadai*]

2 cups mashed potatoes
½ coconut, grated
Crushed red peppers to taste
1¼ teaspoons ground ginger
½ teaspoon ground
  coriander

1 teaspoon ground turmeric
Salt to taste
3 tablespoons rice flour
3 tablespoons lentil flour
Vegetable shortening for
  deep frying

Mix potatoes, coconut, crushed red peppers, ginger, coriander, turmeric, and salt together in mixing bowl. Mix well. Form into small balls. Flatten into small cakes. Combine rice and lentil flour in small bowl. Add just enough water to make a thin batter. Heat vegetable shortening in skillet. Dip potato cakes in batter. Deep-fry. *Yield* 36 potato cakes

STEAMED RICE MUFFINS
[*South Indian Idli*]

½ *cup lentils or black-eyed*   2 *teaspoons salt*
  peas   *Vegetable shortening*
½ *cup raw rice*

Soak lentils and rice for 10 hours in separate bowls. Grind lentils to a fine paste with a little water, adding a little at a time. Use food-chopper fine blade or high-speed blender. Change grinder to coarse blade. Add rice and grind coarsely. Add salt and whip with whisk so that batter gets lighter. Set aside in warm place for 12 hours to facilitate fermentation. Stir batter well. Grease 12 muffin cups or muffin pan. Pour batter into greased cups to ⅔ full. Place in water jacket and cover. Steam batter in cups ½ to ¾ hour. Test for doneness as for cake. Cool. Remove from cups and serve steaming hot with chutney. *Yield* 12 to 15 *idlis*

Note: Farina may be used as a substitute for rice. In this case, farina does not need to be soaked. Mix to a fine paste with a little cold water, and add to fermenting lentil mixture just before steaming.

Finely chopped ginger, onion, crushed red pepper, etc., may be added to mixture just before steaming.

Idlis may be served cold as sandwiches. Cut in fine slices and use chutney as filling.

STEAMED FARINA MUFFINS
[*Soojee Idli*]

½ cup farina
2 tablespoons vegetable
  shortening
½ teaspoon mustard seeds

4 drops hot-pepper sauce
Salt to taste
3 tablespoons grated coconut
1½ cups yogurt

Mix farina to a fine paste with a little water. Heat vegetable shortening in skillet. Add mustard seeds and fry until seeds burst. Add hot-pepper sauce and stir for 1 minute. Pour farina paste into frying spices. Mix for 2 or 3 minutes. Remove skillet from fire. Add salt, coconut, and yogurt; mix well. Grease muffin pan or cups. Pour in batter ⅔ full. Place in water jacket and cover. Steam batter for ½ to ¾ hour. Test for doneness as for cake. Serve hot with chutney. *Yield* 5 small *idlis*

CRISP PUFFS
[*Gol Gappe*]

1 cup whole-wheat flour
Salt to taste
⅛ teaspoon baking powder
Chili powder to taste
1 teaspoon vegetable
  shortening

Vegetable shortening for
  deep frying
2 cups cooked-rhubarb juice
½ teaspoon ground black
  pepper
½ teaspoon ground cumin
Brown sugar to taste

Sift together flour, salt, baking powder, and chili powder. Rub in 1 teaspoon vegetable shortening. Knead, adding just enough water to make a soft dough. Roll out very thin into a big round. Cut into small rounds about 1½ inches in diameter. Heat vegetable shortening for deep frying in large skillet. Deep-fry until light brown. They must be crisp and well bloated. Combine rhubarb juice, pepper, cumin, and brown sugar in pan. Cook for 5 minutes. Mix well. Serve with crisp *gol-gappe*. *Yield* 40 *gol-gappe*

STEAMED CAKE
[Dholka]

¼ cup rice flour
¼ cup lentil flour
4 tablespoons yogurt
⅛ teaspoon ground turmeric
⅛ teaspoon ground fenugreek

Salt to taste
Crushed red peppers to taste
1 teaspoon vegetable
  shortening
¼ cup grated coconut

Combine rice flour, lentil flour, yogurt, turmeric, fenugreek, salt, crushed red peppers, and vegetable shortening in mixing bowl. Mix well. Set aside overnight. Spread out on perforated bottom of steamer. Steam until set. Cut into 12 portions. Sprinkle with coconut. *Yield* 12 *dholka*

COCONUT CAKES
[Narkoler Bara]

2 cups grated coconut
2 tablespoons whole-wheat
  flour
¼ tablespoon anise seeds
¼ teaspoon chili powder

¼ teaspoon salt
Sugar to taste
2 tablespoons vegetable
  shortening

Combine all ingredients, except shortening, in mixing bowl. Mix well. Wet hands. Form into 8 flat cakes. Heat vegetable shortening in skillet. Fry coconut cakes until light brown. *Yield* 8 cakes

MIXED MEATBALLS
[*Queema Goli*]

½ *pound finely minced cooked chicken or duck*
½ *pound finely ground lamb*
1 *medium onion, grated*
¼ *teaspoon crushed red peppers*
¼ *teaspoon ground black pepper*
1 *teaspoon ground turmeric*
½ *teaspoon minced garlic*
1 *tablespoon yogurt*
Salt to taste
Vegetable shortening for deep frying

Combine all ingredients except shortening. Form into 24 small balls. Heat vegetable shortening for deep frying in skillet. Deep-fry balls until brown. Remove and drain. *Yield* 24 meatballs

CURRIED-MEAT TURNOVERS
[*Samosas*]

2 *tablespoons instant minced onion*
2 *tablespoons water*
2 *tablespoons vegetable shortening*
¼ *teaspoon garlic powder*
¼ *teaspoon ground cinnamon*
¼ *teaspoon ground ginger*
¼ *teaspoon cayenne*
2 *teaspoons ground coriander*
¼ *cup chopped fresh tomato*
1½ *cups finely ground lamb or beef*
1¼ *teaspoons salt*
¼ *cup water*
2 *teaspoons fresh lemon juice*
Pastry
Egg white, beaten slightly
Vegetable shortening

Soften onion in the 2 tablespoons water. Sauté in shortening. Add spices and stir and cook 1 minute. Add tomato, beef or lamb, and salt. Stir and cook 2 to 3 minutes. Add water and lemon juice and cook until all liquid is absorbed. Turn out onto a plate to cool.

Roll pastry very thin on a lightly floured board. Cut into circles with a 2½-inch cooky cutter. Brush edges lightly with slightly beaten egg white. Place a rounded ½ teaspoon of the mixture in center of each. Fold over the dough and crimp edges with a fork, being sure they are well sealed. Fry in hot deep vegetable shortening (360° to 375°) until golden brown. Drain on absorbent paper. Serve. *Yield* about 60 turnovers.

SAMOSAS PASTRY

2 *cups sifted all-purpose*
flour
1 *teaspoon salt*

¼ *cup vegetable shortening*
7 *tablespoons yogurt*

Sift flour with salt. Melt vegetable shortening and add to flour. Mix well. Stir in yogurt gradually, working it with hands about 5 minutes. Knead until satiny and smooth. If desired, use your own pastry recipe and bake the puffs in a preheated hot oven (400°) 12 to 15 minutes. *Yield* Pastry for 60 turnovers.

LAMB BALLS
[*Kofta-Sooka*]

1 *pound lamb, finely ground*
1 *small onion, finely chopped*
1 *cup mashed potatoes*
Crushed red peppers to taste
½ *teaspoon ground*
coriander
⅛ *teaspoon ground cloves*
½ *teaspoon ground*
cinnamon

¼ *teaspoon ground black*
pepper
1 *teaspoon ground fennel*
Salt to taste
½ *cup rice flour*
Vegetable shortening for
deep frying

Mix all ingredients except rice flour with meat and potatoes. Make small balls. Roll in rice flour. Heat vegetable shortening in skillet. Fry balls until brown. *Yield* 4 servings

HOT CAKES
[Dosais]

½ cup lentils or split peas
1 cup raw rice

Salt to taste
Vegetable shortening

Soak lentils and rice for 10 hours in separate bowls. Grind lentils and rice to a fine paste with a little water, adding a little at a time. Use food chopper fine blade or high-speed blender. Add salt and whip with whisk so that batter gets lighter. Set aside in warm place for 12 hours to facilitate fermentation. Stir batter well. Add a little water if necessary, to make batter of thin pouring consistency. Heat skillet or griddle and grease evenly with vegetable shortening. Pour batter on griddle and spread batter out to form evenly thin round pancake. Cover with another skillet or any cover that fits over. Not necessary to be tight. Fry for 2 minutes. Uncover. Turn *dosai* over. Cover and fry again for 2 minutes. Remove. Serve hot with chutney. *Yield* 12 to 18 *dosais*

Note: *Thin dosais* do not need covering. Thick *dosais* are cooked better when covered. If you prefer crisper *dosais*, use buttermilk to thin down batter, plus 1 tablespoon (flat) farina to each cup of very thin batter. Allow to soak for one hour. Beat; then use.

POTATO CAKES
[Masalah Dosai]

1 tablespoon vegetable shortening
2 medium onions, finely chopped
¼ teaspoon ground turmeric
Crushed red peppers to taste
1 teaspoon ground ginger
Salt to taste

4 medium potatoes, boiled, cubed
Juice of 1 lime
½ cup lentils, soaked overnight
¾ cup rice, soaked overnight
¼ cup buttermilk to make batter

Heat 1 tablespoon vegetable shortening in large skillet. Add onions. Fry until soft. Add turmeric. Fry for 1 minute. Add crushed red peppers, ginger, salt, and potatoes. Fry until well mixed. Remove. Sprinkle lime juice over potatoes. Place lentils, rice, crushed red peppers, and salt in food chopper. Use fine blade or high-speed blender. Grind to a paste. Beat in rice. Add enough buttermilk to paste to make a pouring consistency. Beat well. Heat griddle or large skillet. Smear with vegetable shortening. Pour ½ of batter to make 4 *dosais*. Fry on both sides. Before removing dosais, add 2 tablespoons of potato mixture. Fold over. Repeat with remaining batter and mixture. *Yield* 8 *dosais*

PUFFED-RICE SALAD
[*Bhel Poori*]

4 cups puffed cereal rice
¼ cup chopped parsley or
  coriander leaves
1 cup diced boiled potatoes
½ cup chopped onion
1 cup crisp broken pooris,
  or saltines

1 lemon, sliced paper thin
½ cup peanuts
½ cup fried chick-peas
2 teaspoons crushed red
  peppers

Place puffed rice, parsley, potatoes, onion, *pooris*, lemon, peanuts and peas in large salad bowl. Toss. Sprinkle peppers over salad. Prepare just before serving so that *pooris* do not lose crispness. *Yield* 4 servings

FARINA SNACK
[*Uppuma*]

¼ cup vegetable shortening
5 sprigs of parsley
½ teaspoon crushed red
  peppers
1 teaspoon cumin seeds
1 teaspoon mustard seeds

1 teaspoon split peas
¼ cup coconut bits
2 cups farina
2 cups buttermilk
1 tablespoon lime juice

Heat vegetable shortening in large skillet. Add parsley and fry crisp. Remove parsley. In same skillet, add crushed red peppers, cumin seeds, mustard seeds, split peas, and coconut. Fry for 2 or 3 minutes. Add farina and fry until light brown. Pour in buttermilk. Do not stir. Cover and cook slowly until farina is dry. Stir lightly with fork. Add lime juice. Garnish with crisp parsley. *Yield* 4 servings

BEAD NECKLACE
[*Muruku*]

2 *cups rice flour*	*Salt water*
1 *cup chick-pea flour*	*Coconut oil*
1 *teaspoon thyme leaves*	*Vegetable shortening for*
3 *tablespoons butter or*	*deep frying*
margarine	

Mix together rice flour, chick-pea flour, and thyme in mixing bowl. Rub in butter or margarine. Knead to a stiff dough using salt water. Smear coconut oil over dough. Cover. Set aside for 1 hour. Heat vegetable shortening for deep frying in skillet. Place part of dough at a time in pastry tube. Use star-shaped end. Squeeze into hot shortening in shape of three-strand necklaces. *Yield* 1 dozen three-strand necklaces

FIGURE-EIGHT CAKES
[*Muruku-Bee Hive*]

1 *teaspoon cumin seeds*	*Salt water*
4 *cups rice flour*	*Coconut oil*
1 *cup lentil flour*	*Vegetable shortening for*
5 *tablespoons butter or*	*deep frying*
margarine	

Combine cumin seeds, rice flour, and lentil flour in mixing bowl. Rub in butter or margarine. Knead to a stiff dough using salt water. Smear dough with coconut oil. Set aside for 1 hour. Heat vegetable shortening for deep frying in skillet. Place small amount of dough at a time in pastry tube. Squeeze figure eights into hot shortening. Deep-fry. Turn once when they rise. *Yield* 3 to 4 dozen

SEASONED LENTILS
[Dal Mote]

1 cup yellow split peas
4 cups water
1 teaspoon soda
Vegetable shortening for
  deep frying

1 tablespoon butter or
  margarine
1 teaspoon curry powder
1 teaspoon salt

Combine split peas and 2 cups of the water and soda. Let soak 12 hours or overnight. Drain and wash thoroughly in cold water. Cover with remaining 2 cups water. Let soak 5 to 6 hours. Drain well and pat peas dry between towels. Fry ¼ cup peas at a time in deep vegetable shortening preheated to 360°. Drain on paper towels. Melt butter or margarine. Add curry powder. Stir. Cook 1 minute. Add to peas along with salt. Mix well. Serve with cocktails. *Yield* 2 cups

CASHEWS
[Bhune Kaju]

2 cups cashew nuts
1½ tablespoons vegetable
  shortening
1 teaspoon salt

¼ teaspoon cayenne
½ teaspoon ground cumin
  seeds

Fry cashew nuts in vegetable shortening until golden brown, about 3 minutes. Drain. Combine salt, cayenne, and cumin and toss with drained nuts. Serve hot or cold with cocktails or as a snack. *Yield* 2 cups

BANANA AND SPINACH FRY
[*Bajji*]

3 cups chick-pea flour
3 teaspoons salt
½ teaspoon ground thyme
½ teaspoon cayenne
1 teaspoon turmeric
Buttermilk
Vegetable shortening for
  deep frying

2 half-ripe unpeeled bananas,
  cut lengthwise in 12 slices
2 medium onions, thick cut
  in 12 slices
12 whole spinach leaves,
  washed and drained

Mix together flour, salt, thyme, cayenne, and turmeric in mixing bowl. Add enough buttermilk to make a thick batter. Heat vegetable shortening for deep frying in skillet. Dip banana pieces in batter to fully coat. Drop in hot shortening, brown 3 at a time, so they can rise. Turn once. Remove and drain. Deep-fry onions, dipped in batter until browned. Remove and drain. Thin out batter. Dip spinach leaves in batter holding by stem. Deep-fry spinach leaves until crisp. Remove and drain. Arrange bananas, onions, and spinach on platter in their own groups. *Yield* 4 servings

TAPIOCA, NUT, AND POTATO FRY
[*Sagoo Khichari*]

½ pound pearl tapioca, soak
  1 hour and drain
2 tablespoon vegetable
  shortening
½ teaspoon cumin seeds
¼ teaspoon crushed red
  peppers

½ cup crushed peanuts
1½ medium potatoes, very
  thinly sliced
⅛ teaspoon salt
¼ teaspoon ground coriander
½ coconut, grated

Heat vegetable shortening in skillet. Add cumin and crushed red peppers. Fry for 2 minutes. Add tapioca, nuts, potatoes, and salt.

Stir well. Cover. Cook slowly for 20 minutes or until tapioca is transparent. Remove from heat. Stir to avoid lumps. Garnish with coriander and coconut. *Yield* 6 servings

SPICED POTATO BALLS
[*Bonda*]

2 *cups hot mashed potatoes*
2 *tablespoons chopped parsley*
1½ *teaspoons ground ginger*
4 *tablespoons chopped pimento*
1 *teaspoon lime juice*
Salt to taste
1 *tablespoon vegetable shortening*

1 *teaspoon mustard seeds*
2 *teaspoons lentils*
¼ *cup rice flour*
¼ *cup chick-pea flour*
1 *teaspoon salt*
¼ *teaspoon cayenne*
4 *tablespoons vegetable shortening*

Mix together potatoes, parsley, ginger, pimento, lime juice, and salt to taste in mixing bowl. Heat 1 tablespoon vegetable shortening in large round spoon. Add mustard seeds and lentils. Fry until mustard seeds stop sputtering. Add to potatoes and mix with same spoon. Mix together flours, 1 teaspoon salt, and cayenne on flat dish. Wet hand and form potatoes into large-shaped marbles. Keep ball surface wet. Roll in flour. Heat vegetable shortening in skillet. Fry potato balls a few at a time. Tilt can so balls rotate and fry brown evenly all over. Remove and drain. *Yield* 4 to 6 servings

SAVORY POTATO STRAWS
[*Alu Ke Lachche*]

2 *medium-size potatoes*
Vegetable shortening for deep frying

½ *teaspoon salt*
¾ *teaspoon ground caraway*
1/16 *teaspoon cayenne*

Peel, wash, and shred potatoes. Drain and dry. Fry in hot deep vegetable shortening (375°) 3 to 5 minutes or until golden brown.

Remove from vegetable shortening and drain. Combine salt and spices and mix with drained potatoes. Serve with cocktails. *Yield* about 2 cups

POTATO BASKETS
[*Aloo*]

1 *pound potatoes, peeled*	*Salt to taste*
Vegetable shortening for	
deep frying	

Grate potatoes. Place grated potatoes on towel. Squeeze out moisture. Line a small-size strainer with grated potatoes. Press a smaller strainer inside to keep potatoes in position. Heat vegetable shortening for deep frying in large skillet. Dip strainers in hot shortening. Fry until potatoes are golden brown. Turn out. Dust with salt. Repeat until all potatoes are used up. *Yield* 8 baskets

Note: Baskets may be filled with meats or vegetables.

Desserts:
Halwa, Barfi, and Sweetmeats

CARROT HALWA
[Kazaar]

¾ cup milk, divided
2 cups hot mashed carrots
½ cup sugar
¼ tablespoon ground mace
½ tablespoon saffron

¼ tablespoon ground cardamom
8 tablespoons sweet butter, divided

Pour ½ cup milk in saucepan and heat. Add carrots slowly until thick. Keep stirring. Add sugar slowly until dissolved in carrots. Combine ¼ cup milk, mace, saffron, and cardamom in small saucepan and warm. Add slowly to carrots to thicken. Divide butter in four. Add butter a little at a time stirring after each addition; wait until butter has been absorbed before adding more butter. After last butter has been added keep stirring until the *kazaar* appears shiny. Turn onto flat dish. Serve. *Yield* 6 to 8 servings

EGG HALWA
[Andonka Halwa]

1 can (15 ounces) sweetened condensed milk
8 eggs, beaten
½ cup sweet butter
1 tablespoon finely ground almonds

1 tablespoon sliced almonds
2 tablespoons sliced pistachios
1½ teaspoons ground cardamom

Place milk, eggs, butter, and almonds in saucepan. Cook on low heat, continually stirring. Cook until *halwa* begins to come off sides of pan. Garnish with pistachios and cardamom. *Yield* 4 servings

BOMBAY HALWA

2⅔ cups farina, soaked in
water for 5 hours
4 cups sugar
2 cups sweet butter

½ cup blanched almonds,
sliced
1¼ teaspoons ground
cardamom
2 tablespoons rose water

Drain farina through a cloth. Place in pan. Add sugar. Cook over moderate heat stirring all the time. When half cooked, add butter, a little at a time. Keep stirring until thick. Add almonds, cardamom, and rose water. Remove from heat. Grease large dish. Turn *halwa* onto dish. Cool. Cut as desired. *Yield* 20 pieces

NUT AND SAFFRON HALWA
[*Badami Halwa*]

1 cup sugar
1 cup water
1 cup flour
¼ cup sweet butter

½ teaspoon saffron, soaked
in 1 tablespoon water
12 almonds, finely grated
12 pistachios, finely grated

Place sugar and water in saucepan. Boil 5 minutes. Add flour. Cook until thick. Add butter, a little at a time. Keep stirring until *halwa* leaves sides of pan. Add saffron. Mix well. Pour on large dish. Cool. Sprinkle with almonds and pistachios. Cut in diamonds. *Yield* 20 pieces

CARDAMOM AND ALMOND HALWA
[*Mahim Halwa*]

1 *cup flour*
3 *cups sugar*
1 *cup water*
3 *cups sweet butter, divided*

2 *tablespoons sliced blanched almonds*
½ *teaspoon ground cardamom*

Combine flour, sugar, and water in saucepan. Cook slowly. Add 1 cup butter, stirring all the time. Slowly add remaining butter. Continue cooking. When butter begins to separate and mixture forms a ball, remove from heat. Spread on greased flat pan. Flatten to a thin layer. Sprinkle on almonds and cardamom. Cut into 4-inch by 4-inch squares. *Yield* 12 pieces

TAPIOCA HALWA
[*Sagoo Halwa*]

2 *cups pearl tapioca*
2 *cups thick coconut milk*
½ *cup sugar*
½ *cup water*
4 *tablespoons butter*

1 *teaspoon saffron*
1 *teaspoon ground cardamom*
¼ *cup unsalted chopped cashew nuts*

Combine tapioca and coconut milk in bowl. Allow to soak for 1 hour. Pour into high-speed blender and grind. Combine sugar and water in large saucepan. Cover. Boil 5 minutes. Add tapioca, butter, saffron, and cardamom. Cook, stirring, until mixture leaves sides of pan. Pour in greased dish or pan. Sprinkle on nuts. Press nuts down. Cool. Cut in squares. *Yield* 1½ dozen

SWEET PUFFS
[Khaja]

1 cup flour	½ cup sugar
1/16 teaspoon salt	¼ cup water
2 tablespoons farina	Vegetable shortening for
1 cup rose water	deep frying
3 tablespoons vegetable	¾ teaspoon ground
shortening, divided	cardamom
2 tablespoons flour	1 tablespoon crushed
½ cup dry powdered milk	pistachios
¼ cup heavy cream	

Place 1 cup flour, salt, and farina in mixing bowl. Rub in 2 tablespoons of vegetable shortening. Add rose water. Knead to a
smooth soft dough. Roll out dough very thin. Blend together 1
tablespoon vegetable shortening and 2 tablespoons flour. Beat,
until light. Spread lightly over rolled-out dough. Sprinkle water
evenly all over. Roll up and twist roll. Chill in refrigerator 1 hour.
Blend together powdered milk and cream. Knead to a soft dough.
Reserve. Combine sugar and water in saucepan. Cover. Boil 5
minutes. Remove and reserve. Divide dough roll into 2-inch pieces.
Press down vertically and roll out about size of a saucer. Place a
spoonful of milk-and-cream dough in the center of a rolled-out
round. Cover with another round. Dampen edges and stick together. Heat vegetable shortening for deep frying in skillet. Deep-
fry stuffed round until crisp and brown. Press down lightly during
frying to help it bloat up. Remove and drain. Place on platter.
Pour sugar syrup over *khaja*. Sprinkle with cardamom and pistachios. *Yield* 4 to 6 servings

SWEET DOUGH BALLS
[*Jeebe Gaja*]

½ cup flour
⅛ teaspoon baking powder
1/16 teaspoon salt
1 tablespoon vegetable
 shortening

½ cup sugar
¼ cup water
Vegetable shortening for
 deep frying

Sift together flour, baking powder, and salt. Rub 1 tablespoon of vegetable shortening in flour. Knead with enough water to make a soft dough. Divide dough into 16 balls. Roll each ball to a thin oblong shape. Prick with fork. Combine sugar and water. Cover. Boil 5 minutes. Remove syrup from heat. Heat vegetable shortening for deep frying in skillet. Place each ball in hot vegetable shortening. Fry until light brown and crisp. Soak in syrup. *Yield* 16 dough balls

CASHEW AND COCONUT SWEET
[*Manohara*]

3 cups unsalted cashew nuts
Milk
1½ cups grated coconut
1½ cups boiling water
4 cups powdered sugar

1 tablespoon vanilla
1 tablespoon crushed
 cardamom
2 tablespoons sweet butter

Soak cashew nuts in just enough milk to dampen. Place coconut and cashew nuts in food chopper. Grind to a paste. Pour water in saucepan. Boil. Add sugar. Cook syrup until it threads. Add paste, vanilla, cardamom, and butter. Cook, stirring until sweet leaves sides of pan. Roll like dough. Grease platter. Pat sweet onto platter. Cut when cool. *Yield* 2½ to 3 dozen

THICK SWEET CREAM
[*Basoondi*]

4 cups milk
2 cups sugar
1 tablespoon grated pistachio
nuts

1 tablespoon grated almonds
¼ teaspoon ground nutmeg

Pour milk in large pan. Bring to a boil. Add sugar. Boil until reduced to 2 cups. Keep stirring while boiling. When fairly thick, remove and cool. Garnish with nuts and nutmeg. *Yield* 4 servings

SWEETMEATS
[*Rasogolla*]

1 cup unsalted farmer cheese
1 teaspoon farina
Sugar-cube pieces

4 cups sugar
2 cups water
½ teaspoon rose water

Drain all water from cheese, and cream cheese and farina to a smooth paste. Divide into 15 small balls. Fill each ball with a cube of sugar. Combine sugar and water in saucepan. Cover. Boil 5 minutes. Divide syrup in half. Continue boiling ½ of sugar, adding water to avoid thickening. Drop in balls gently. Cook till balls float under surface of syrup. Drain balls. Place in other ½ of syrup and soak. Remove and cool. Sprinkle with rose water. *Yield* 15 pieces

FRIED CREAM BALLS
[*Gokul Pithe*]

½ cup dry powdered milk
¼ cup heavy cream
1 cup grated coconut
3 teaspoons sugar
½ teaspoon ground
   cardamom
½ cup flour

1/16 teaspoon salt
½ cup milk
½ cup sugar
¼ cup water
Vegetable shortening for
   deep frying

Blend together powdered milk and cream. Knead to a soft dough. Place in saucepan. Add coconut, sugar, and cardamom. Heat until mixture holds together. Allow to cool. Shape into 20 small flat balls. Reserve. Sift together flour and salt in mixing bowl. Add milk slowly. Beat for a few minutes until batter is well mixed. Combine sugar and water in separate saucepan. Cover. Boil for 5 minutes. Heat vegetable shortening for deep frying in skillet. Dip small balls in batter. Place in hot vegetable shortening. Fry until golden brown. Remove and drain. Dip in sugar syrup. Place on rack to drain. *Yield 20 pithes*

NUT-AND-RAISIN DESSERT
[*Phirini*]

2 cups milk
2 tablespoons rice flour
½ cup sugar
2 teaspoons blanched
   almonds

2 teaspoons pistachios
1 tablespoon vegetable
   shortening
2 teaspoons raisins
½ teaspoon rose water

Bring milk to boil. Add rice flour and sugar and cook slowly, stirring all the time until it thickens. Fry almonds and pistachios in vegetable shortening until light brown. Remove nuts, place in raisins and fry for a minute. Pour dessert into serving dishes and garnish with almonds, pistachios, and raisins. Sprinkle with rose water. *Yield* 3 to 4 servings

VERMICELLI DESSERT
[*Seviyan*]

¼ cup sweet butter
2 cups broken finest
  vermicelli
1 tablespoon rose water

¼ cup honey
2 tablespoons sugar
2 tablespoons hot water

Heat butter in flat Pyrex dish. Add vermicelli. Stir to coat all vermicelli. Place in 350° oven to fry slightly. Combine rose water, honey, sugar, and hot water in top of double boiler. Stir until all ingredients are blended. Sprinkle syrup over vermicelli. Cover. Place in 350° oven for 20 minutes or until tender. *Yield* 4 to 6 servings

GOLDEN-FRIED BREAD IN CREAM SAUCE
[*Shahi Turka*]

⅛ teaspoon saffron
1 teaspoon water
12 slices bread, ½ inch thick
⅔ cup vegetable shortening
¾ cup sugar
½ cup water

⅛ teaspoon ground
  cardamom
1 cup heavy cream
Indian silver-leaf paper
  (optional)
2 tablespoons slivered
  blanched almonds

Dissolve saffron in the 1 teaspoon water and set aside to use later. Purchase day-old sliced bread. Trim crust from bread and cut slices into pieces 3 by 4 inches. Melt shortening slowly in a 9-

or 10-inch skillet. Skim off foam and discard it. Add bread slices to hot shortening (only enough to cover bottom of pan at one time) and sauté until all bread is golden brown, turning to brown both sides. Repeat until all bread has been browned. Combine sugar and water in a small saucepan. Mix well. Bring to boiling point and boil 5 minutes or until syrup begins to thicken. Add dissolved saffron, cardamom, and cream. Mix well. Bring to boiling point and boil 1 minute. Pour over fried bread. Let stand until cold, turning to soak both sides. Place 2 slices in each of 6 fruit dishes with some of the sauce spooned over each serving. Top each with Indian silver-leaf paper and slivered blanched almonds. If silver leaf is not available, top dessert with whipped cream if desired. *Yield* 6 servings

NUT AND RAISIN DESSERT
[Zarda]

3 tablespoons vegetable
  shortening
1 cup half-cooked rice
1/16 teaspoon salt
3 cardamom, coarsely crushed
1 stick cinnamon, 1 inch
  long, crushed
1 cup milk
4 tablespoons sugar
2 tablespoons heavy cream

½ teaspoon saffron, crushed
  and soaked in 2 tablespoons
  of warm milk
1 teaspoon lime juice
2 tablespoons blanched and
  sliced almonds
2 tablespoons raisins
2 tablespoons blanched and
  sliced pistachios

Heat shortening in frying pan that has cover. Add rice, salt, crushed cardamom, cinnamon, and fry for a few minutes. Add milk and sugar and cover pan until rice is cooked. Add cream and mix all ingredients in pan. Sprinkle saffron and lime juice over rice mixture. Cover and cook for one or two minutes. Serve garnished with almonds, raisins, and pistachios. *Yield* 4 servings

CASHEW SWEET
[*Mysore Barfi*]

1 *cup unsalted cashew nuts*	2 *tablespoons sweet butter*
Milk to dampen nuts	1 *tablespoon ground*
2 *cups milk*	*cardamom*
3 *cups powdered sugar*	½ *tablespoon ground mace*

Soak cashew nuts in just enough milk to dampen. Place in food chopper and grind. Pour milk in saucepan. Add sugar, ground cashew nuts, and butter. Cook slowly until sweet leaves sides of pan. Turn onto greased platter. Sprinkle cardamom and mace over sweet. Press in gently. Cut when cool. *Yield 1½ to 2 dozen*

RICE AND COCONUT SWEET
[*Prathaman*]

2 *cups grated coconut*	2 *mashed bananas*
2 *tablespoons rice flour*	½ *cup sliced mixed nuts*
2 *cups powdered sugar, brown*	4 *tablespoons sweet butter*
⅛ *teaspoon ground*	⅛ *teaspoon powdered ginger*
cardamom	

Combine coconut and flour. Place all ingredients in saucepan. Cook slowly until sweet leaves sides of pan. Turn onto greased platter. Cut when cool. *Yield 1 to 1½ dozen*

CHOCOLATE SWEET
[*Cocoa Barfi*]

1⅓ *cups powdered dry milk*	1½ *teaspoons ground*
⅔ *cup heavy cream*	*cardamom*
1 *cup sugar*	1 *tablespoon cocoa*
	1 *tablespoon milk*

Blend together powdered milk and cream. Knead to soft dough.
Place in saucepan over low heat. Add sugar. Blend together, stirring until mixture comes off from sides of pan. Add cardamom.
Mix well. Turn onto a greased flat cake tin. Cool and allow to
set. In same saucepan add cocoa and milk. Cook slowly until it
forms a paste. Spread a thin layer on the *barfi*. Cut into diamonds. *Yield 20 barfi*

MOON CAKES
[*Chandra Puli*]

½ cup dry powdered milk
1 cup unsalted farmer cheese
2 cups sugar, divided
¼ cup water

1 cup finely grated coconut
1 tablespoon ground
  cardamom

Combine powdered milk, cheese, and ½ cup sugar in mixing
bowl. Knead until well blended. Reserve. Combine 1½ cups sugar
and water in saucepan. Heat until soft-ball stage. Grind coconut
to a paste. Add to sugar. Stir until thickened and it begins to
stick to pan. Add milk-and-cheese mixture. Keep stirring until it
leaves sides of pan. Turn onto greased paper or pan. Mold into
cresent-shaped moons. Sprinkle with cardamom and press in. Dry.
Yield 1½ dozen

SWEET CAKE
[*Gauja*]

1 cup flour
1/16 teaspoon salt
2 teaspoons vegetable
  shortening
1 cup sugar

½ cup water
Vegetable shortening for
  deep frying
1 teaspoon ground
  cardamom

Sift together flour and salt. Rub 2 teaspoons of vegetable shortening into flour. Knead to a soft dough. Divide into 14 parts. Roll

each into thin pancake. Make slits in center making sure that ends are not separated. Hold ends and twist. Combine sugar and water in saucepan. Cover. Boil 5 minutes. Remove and reserve. Heat vegetable shortening for deep frying in skillet. Place twisted dough in skillet. Fry until brown. Remove and drain. Dip in sugar syrup for a few minutes. Remove. Sprinkle with cardamom. Yield 14 *gauja.*

POTATO SWEET
[*Ranga-Aloor-Puli*]

1 cup hot mashed sweet
  potatoes
1½ tablespoons flour
Pinch of salt

2 cups sugar
1 cup water
Vegetable shortening for
  deep frying

Combine potatoes, flour, and salt in mixing bowl. Knead to a soft dough. Combine sugar and water in saucepan. Cover. Boil 5 minutes. Reduce heat and keep warm. Divide potato dough into small balls. Flatten into semicircular shapes. Heat vegetable shortening for deep frying in skillet. Deep-fry *puli* until golden brown. Remove and drain. Soak in hot syrup. Cool. Yield 12 pieces

SUGAR SQUASH
[*Cheenee Kuddoo*]

1 cup sugar
¼ cup boiling water
¼ teaspoon ground
  cardamom
½ cup unsalted cashew nuts
¼ cup grated coconut
2 teaspoons salt
2 teaspoons cayenne

2 teaspoons ground turmeric
2 tablespoons chick-pea flour
1½ cups yogurt
4 cups cubed squash, ½-inch
  squares
Vegetable shortening for
  deep frying

Place sugar in saucepan over low heat. Stir constantly 8 to 10 minutes until sugar is melted and smoking. Sugar should be straw-colored. Remove from heat. Add boiling water slowly, stirring as you add to avoid spattering and lumps. Heat again 8 to 10 minutes until deep brown. Add cardamom, cashew nuts, and coconut. Place pan in another larger pan containing boiling water to keep syrup warm. Combine salt, cayenne, turmeric, and chick-pea flour in large bowl. Add yogurt to spices to make batter. Add squash to batter. Mix squash to coat with batter. Heat vegetable shortening for deep frying in skillet. Deep-fry squash until browned. Remove and drain. Place on serving dish. Pour warm syrup with nuts over squash. *Yield* 4 servings

PAYASAM

1 *quart coconut milk*	1 *cup vermicelli, not too fine*
¾ *cup sugar*	2 *tablespoons sweet butter*
1 *teaspoon ground*	¼ *cup crushed cashew nuts*
cardamom	1 *teaspoon rose water*
3 *cups water*	

Combine coconut milk, sugar, and cardamom in large saucepan. Slowly simmer. Add water to a separate large saucepan and bring to a boil. Add vermicelli. Stir with a fork. When water comes to a rolling boil again, remove and drain. Add vermicelli to simmering coconut milk. Lightly loosen with fork all the vermicelli. Heat butter in small skillet. Shake in cashew nuts. Fry until slightly discolored. Add to cooking vermicelli. Wait 2 minutes. Remove pan from heat. Add rose water. Cover pan. Serve cold. *Yield* 4 servings

NUT SWEETS
[*Mohan Thal*]

2 cups sugar
¾ cup water
1 cup chick-pea flour
¼ cup milk
2 tablespoons butter or
    margarine
½ cup vegetable shortening

¾ teaspoon ground
    cardamom
2 tablespoons finely sliced
    pistachios
2 tablespoons finely sliced
    blanched almonds

Combine sugar and water in saucepan. Cover. Boil 5 minutes. Reserve. Place chick-pea flour, milk, and 2 tablespoons butter or margarine in mixing bowl. Blend. Heat ½ cup vegetable shortening in skillet. Add flour mixture. Fry until golden brown. Add sugar syrup. Mix well. Cook until mixture swells. Turn onto flat tray and allow to set. Sprinkle on cardamom. Garnish with pistachios and almonds. Cut into diamonds. *Yield* 16 pieces

SWEETMEATS IN SYRUP
[*Gulab Jammun*]

2 cups dry powdered milk
½ teaspoon cooking soda
2 tablespoons flour
2 tablespoons rose water
1 cup heavy sweet cream
2 tablespoons sugar

2 tablespoons ground
    cardamom
4 cups sugar
⅔ cup water
3 tablespoons vegetable
    shortening

Sift together powdered milk, soda, and flour into mixing bowl. Add rose water, then cream, slowly kneading to a stiff dough. Form into walnut-size round balls. Mix together sugar and carda-

mom. Make hole in dough ball with thumb. Pour in small amount
of sugar and cardamom. Close up hole. Combine sugar and water
in saucepan. Cover. Boil 5 minutes. Reserve and keep hot. Heat
vegetable shortening in skillet. Fry balls until well browned. Remove and drain. Soak in hot syrup. *Yield* 2 dozen

SWEETMEAT
[*Sandesh*]

3½ cups unsalted farmer   ½ teaspoon ground
   cheese or ricotta cheese   cardamom
1½ cups sugar, powdered

Rub cheese until smooth. Place in saucepan. Mix in sugar. Heat,
stirring all the time until mixture leaves sides of pan. Add cardamom. Remove from heat. Turn onto flat dish or tray. Form into
desired shapes while mixture is hot. *Yield* 24 pieces

ALMOND SWEET
[*Tirangi Mithai*]

1 cup ground almonds   1 teaspoon saffron, soaked
1 tablespoon rose water   in 1 tablespoon water
½ cup sugar   1 tablespoon grated coconut
½ cup sweet butter   ½ teaspoon ground
                           cardamom

Place almonds, rose water, and sugar in saucepan. Heat until
well mixed. Slowly add butter until mixture begins to come off
from sides of pan. Divide mixture in three. Mix saffron in one
mixture. Mix coconut in another. Leave third mixture. Spread
each mixture on a greased flat dish, one on top of another. Sprinkle
on cardamom. Cut in diamonds. *Yield* 20 pieces

NUT SWEET
[Mysore Pak]

1½ cups sweet butter
⅔ cup chick-pea flour
1¼ cups sugar
⅔ cup water
1 teaspoon baking soda

1 teaspoon nutmeg, ground
½ teaspoon mace, ground
1 tablespoon finely chopped
   almonds

Place butter in pan and melt. Keep hot. Do not brown. Place chick-pea flour in mixing bowl. Rub in 2 tablespoons of warm butter. Combine sugar and water in saucepan. Cover. Boil 5 minutes. Add flour mixture to syrup. Stir well to avoid lumps. Add remaining hot butter a spoonful at a time, stirring constantly until all the butter has been used up and surface appears rough. Add baking soda before pouring. Pour mixture immediately into a flat pan to make 1½-inch-thick layer. Sprinkle spices. Press down the nuts with flat spoon. Set at an angle to drain off extra butter. Garnish with nuts. Cut into squares or diamonds. *Yield* 20 pieces

Note: for *Mysore Pak:* 1. Syrup should be thready when poured from spoon.
2. Add butter-rubbed flour all at once.
3. Keep 4 tablespoons of butter-rubbed flour in reserve. This is to sprinkle on the mixture if it seems to bubble too much, yet not rolling off sides of pan.

NUT SWEETS
[Dil-Pasand]

¼ teaspoon saffron
1 tablespoon hot milk
½ pound unsalted almonds
   or cashew nuts
½ cup rose water
1½ cups sugar

1½ cups water
1 cup sweet butter
2 tablespoons grated unsalted
   pistachios
1 teaspoon ground
   cardamom

Place saffron in milk. Crush and set aside. Grind together to a paste, almonds and rose water in food chopper. Use fine blade or high-speed blender. Place sugar and water in saucepan. Boil for 5 minutes. Add nut paste. Cook until thick. Add butter, stirring constantly. When butter begins to separate, add saffron. Mix well. Remove from heat. Spread out on plate thickly. Sprinkle with pistachios and cardamom. Cut into squares when half set. *Yield* 14 pieces

SWEET FRIED CAKES
[Amriti]

1 cup lentils, soaked 4 hours
1 teaspoon saffron
Vegetable shortening for
   deep frying
5 cups sugar

3 cups water
1 tablespoon milk
⅛ teaspoon yellow vegetable
   coloring

Place lentils and saffron in food chopper. Use fine blade or high-speed blender. Grind to a paste. Add just enough water to make thick consistency. Beat well until fluffy. Fill pastry tube, with ¼-inch hole, with lentil batter. Heat vegetable shortening for deep frying in skillet. Squeeze out batter, making circular design in hot shortening. Fry until lightly browned. Combine sugar, water, milk, and coloring in large pan. Heat until syrup begins to boil. Remove. Dip hot *amriti* in hot syrup. Soak for 2 minutes. Drain. *Yield* 40 *amriti*

SWEET NUT BALLS
[*Kin Quab "Little Dream"*]

4 *tablespoons sweet butter,*	¼ *cup rice flour*
divided	½ *cup blanched grated*
1 *cup powdered sugar*	*almonds*
¼ *cup poppy seeds*	½ *cup unsalted chopped*
4 *cups crumbled sweet*	*cashew nuts*
wafers	½ *cup raisins*
1 *tablespoon rose water*	

Cream together 2 tablespoons butter and sugar. Add poppy seeds. Beat together until fluffy. Fold in sweet wafers and rose water. Heat 2 tablespoons butter in skillet. Add rice flour, almonds, cashew nuts, and raisins. Fry 1 or 2 minutes. Add to sweet-wafer mixture. Mix well. Shape into small balls. *Yield* approximately 3 dozen

SWEET CUBES
[*Dilkush*]

1 *cup farina*	2 *cups powdered sugar*
2 *cups sweet butter*	1 *cup thick coconut milk*
1 *cup chick-pea flour*	½ *tablespoon ground*
6 *cashew nuts*	*cardamom*
1 *cup milk*	

Place farina in mixing bowl. Add just enough water to cover. Soak for ½ hour. Add ½ cup water. Knead farina into spongy ball. Squeeze out water. Reserve farina and farina water. Rub 3 tablespoons of butter into chick-pea flour. Heat remaining butter in large skillet. Add cashew nuts. Fry 2 or 3 minutes. Add chick-pea flour. Crumble reserved farina and add to skillet. Fry, sprinkling with milk, until cooked and gold-colored. Add sugar. Mix well. Add coconut milk and reserved farina water. Stir until mixture thickens. Add cardamom. Cook until mixture leaves sides of pan. Turn onto platter. Cut in cubes when lukewarm. *Yield* 10 to 12 servings

SWEET MILK BALLS
[*Paal Kozukatai*]

4 tablespoons sweet butter
1 cup farina
2 tablespoons ground
 cardamom, divided

2 cups milk
2 cups powdered sugar,
 divided
4 cups thick coconut milk

Rub butter into farina. Add 1 tablespoon cardamom. Blend in. Pour milk in saucepan. Add farina. Stir briskly. Remove from heat. Stir in 1 cup of sugar. Quickly roll farina into olive-sized balls. Pour coconut milk in saucepan. Add 1 cup sugar and 1 tablespoon cardamom. Bring to a boil. Place in balls. Simmer for 5 minutes. Cool before serving. *Yield* 1 to 1½ dozen

PANCAKE SWEET
[*Malpura*]

¾ cup sugar
1 cup water
1 teaspoon saffron
2 cups sifted flour
2 tablespoons farina

1 teaspoon baking powder
12 almonds, finely chopped
½ cup raisins
Milk

Combine sugar and water in saucepan. Cover. Boil 5 minutes. Add saffron. Remove from heat. Cool. Add flour, farina, baking powder, almonds, and raisins. Beat well. Add just enough milk to make light-batter consistency. Heat griddle. Smear with butter. Ladle batter onto griddle so that nut and fruits are distributed. Brown on both sides. *Yield* 2 dozen

FRUIT AND NUT CAKE
[*Sooji Cake*]

2 cups seedless raisins
4 tablespoons chopped
  crystallized ginger
¼ cup miced orange peel
¼ cup minced lime peel
¾ pound almonds, chopped
2 tablespoons rose water
4 tablespoons rum
1½ teaspoons ground nutmeg

1 teaspoon ground
  cardamom
1 teaspoon caraway seeds
1 teaspoon ground mace
1⅓ cups farina
1½ cups butter
2¼ cups sugar, divided
6 egg whites
6 egg yolks
4 tablespoons wheat flour

Two weeks before baking, take a large jar with tight lid and place in the following: raisins, ginger, orange peel, lime peel, almonds, rose water, rum, nutmeg, cardamom, caraway, and mace. Tighten lid. Shake well to mix all ingredients thoroughly. Reserve for 2 weeks. Place farina in large bowl. Cut in butter. Reserve for 1 hour. Beat egg whites with 1 cup plus 2 tablespoons sugar. Beat egg yolks with remaining sugar. Turn egg yolks and whites into large bowl. Beat in farina. Reserve for ½ hour. Add contents of jar in small scoops, beating in each addition. Sprinkle with flour after each scoop of mixture from jar is beaten. Pour in cake pan that will fit in larger pan. Add water to larger pan. Cover pans over tightly with foil. Steam for 2 hours. Uncover. Place in 325° oven for 45 minutes or until top browns. *Yield* 1 cake

Tea

Tea customs in India, one of the world's largest tea-producing countries, still bear the influence of their English cousins.

A refreshing cup of tea is usually taken upon rising, again at breakfast, midmorning, four in the afternoon, and frequently as a soothing beverage at bedtime.

Tea is served "neat" or with sugar and milk. Cream is never used because it "coats" the flavor of tea. Essential techniques for brewing a "proper cup of tea" to refresh the inner man and mind are inherent.

In remote rural areas in India, tea is often brewed in a pan called a *dekchi*. The water is brought to a boil in the pan, over a *chula* or open fire. Tea leaves are added, and a tight lid put on for the brewing period. A brass ladle is used to pour the tea into undecorated mugs or unglazed clay bowls called *khulahs*.

Glossary

Akhni or *Yakhni*—Soup or stock.

Aloo—Potato.

Amriti—A sweetmeat.

Atla—Whole-meal flour.

Baffat—A curry with meat and radishes.

Baghar—Tempering done after the dish has been prepared. Onions and a few spices or herbs are fried in a spoonful of fat and added to the cooked dish to improve flavoring.

Balushai—A round ball made of dough slightly flattened at the center, fried and dipped in sugar syrup.

Barfi—A fudgelike sweet.

Basundi—Milk sweet.

Bhaji—Another term for vegetable preparations.

Bhajja—Slices of vegetables dipped in lentil-flour batter and fried crisp.

Bhel puri—Crisp-fried thin rounds of dough mixed with puffed rice, fried lentils, chopped onion, herbs, and chutney.

Bhindi—An Indian vegetable known as lady's finger or okra.

Bhujia—A North Indian vegetable preparation.

Bhurta—Vegetable boiled or roasted in charcoal, peeled, mashed and sautéed with a little chopped onion and chilies.

Biryani—A rich preparation of rice. Three fourths boiled rice is put in layers with a rich meat or vegetable curry and the whole is baked until done.

Black peppercorn—The berry of the pepper vine dried with the skin on.

Bonda—Mashed potatoes, seasoned and formed into balls, dipped in batter and deep fried—a South Indian snack.

Bouquet garni—A bunch of herbs or spices used for flavoring.

Brinjal—Eggplant.

Cardamon—A spice—the fruit of the cardamom tree. The seeds are found in a pod which is dried. It has a pleasing taste and flavor.

Chapati or *phulka*—Wheat bread made of unfermented dough, round in shape and paper thin. Resembles *tortilla*.

Charoli—An Indian nut.

Chikoo—A brown Indian fruit—a cross between a fig and a russet apple.

Chiwda—A mixture of nuts, fried pressed rice, fried lentils, gram preparation, and spices.

Coriander—A spice. The seed of a small herb.

Cumin—A spice resembling caraway seed.

Curry powder— A mixture of various spices such as coriander, chilies, turmeric, cumin, etc., roasted and powdered together.

Custard apple—Resembles a leaf artichoke—luscious custardlike fruit with hard black stone inside.

Dahi—Yogurt.

Dahibara—Ground lentils, made into fried balls and then steeped in seasoned, beaten yogurt. Served with *pulao* or as a snack.

Dal—Lentil. There is a large variety of lentils in India.

Dhan sak—A Parsee preparation made of rice and curry.

Doodh pak—Sweetmeats made of rice and milk.

Do pyaza—A meat preparation. Onion is added twice, fried and ground. Hence: *do*—twice, and *pyaz*—onion.

Dosa—A type of savory pancake made with fermented batter of ground lentils and rice. A specialty of the South.

Dum—A process of cooking with heat from above as well as below.

Firnee—A creamy milk pudding made of rice flour.

Garam masalah—A mixture of cloves, cinnamon, cardamom, pepper, and cumin.

Gaujas—A fancy sweetmeat made of dough fried and dipped in sugar syrup.

Ghee—Clarified butter or vegetable shortening processed to resemble clarified butter.

Gram—A variety of lentil. Split peas, chick-peas, or green peas are often used as a substitute. Flour is also made from the dry lentil or pea.

Groundnut—Peanut.

Guava—A popular fruit used to make guava cheese, jelly, and stewed fruit.

Gulab jamun—A milk sweetmeat, made of *khoa*.

Halwa—A sweet dish made of lentils, farina or wheat, or of vegetables such as beetroot, carrot, and pumpkin, with butter, milk, and sugar.

Hopper—A griddlecake made of fermented batter. It is eaten with stew.

Idli—A fermented batter of ground lentils and rice steamed in molds; a specialty of South India.

Jaggery—Refined and solidified molasses.

Jalebi—A golden-colored crisp sweet filled with sugar syrup formed in rings.

Kebabs—A savory barbecue done on a skewer. Pieces of meat or minced meat are used.

Kalia—A Bengali vegetable preparation with spices and yogurt.

Keema—Minced meat.

Kesari—A South Indian sweet dish made of vermicelli or farina.

Kheer—A puddinglike preparation of milk and other ingredients.

Khichri—Mixture of rice and lentils.

Khoa—Milk is boiled down till all moisture is removed, used as a base for a large number of Indian sweets.

Kofta—Minced meatball.

Korma—A thick meat curry enriched with ground poppy seeds and desiccated coconut.

Laddoo—A sweet ball of split-pea or lentil flour, rice or farina, sweetened with sugar or molasses.

Lassi—A beverage made of beaten yogurt diluted with water. Sugar or salt may be added.

Lichi—A luscious fruit. It looks like a bigger version of strawberry and is grown in Bengal, Dehra Dun, and Delhi regions.

Loochi—Bengal version of *poori*.

Machher jhol—Bengali fish preparation.

Machhi—Fish.

Mango—A luscious fruit which has several varieties—Dasehri Chausa, Langra, Alfonso, etc.

Maida—Refined flour.

Maize—Indian corn.

Marinate—To steep in a mixture of yogurt or vinegar to soften.

Masalah—Indian condiments and spices.

Mattar—Peas.

Mawa—Same as Khoa—Milk, evaporated to remove all moisture.

Moilee—Fish or prawn cooked in plenty of coconut milk—mildly spiced.

Murgh musallam—A spicy chicken preparation.

Nan roti—Indian bread made of slightly leavened dough baked in a mud oven built into the wall.

Neera—A nonfermented drink obtained from coconut palm.

Pachadi—Seasoned yogurt with vegetables—served in South India.

Pani puri—A puff of dough fried and eaten with tamarind water and sprouted gram.

Panir—Cottage cheese made by curdling milk with lemon juice and straining whey.

Papad (Northern India)

Papadum (Southern India)—A crisp spiced wafer made from rice or gram flour.

Papaya—A luscious tropical fruit.

Paratha—Fried bread made of unleavened wheat flour.

Payasam—A South Indian milk pudding made from vermicelli or lentils.

Pomfret—A type of whitefish very popular in Bombay.

Poori—Deep-fried, round wheat bread.

Pulao—Rice preparation. Rice is fried in fat and cooked in stock and water.

Pulao Rice—A special type of rice used in *pulao*—thin and long, not as starchy as ordinary rice.

Rabri—Sweet, thickened milk.

Raita—Vegetable, raw or parboiled, mixed with beaten and seasoned yogurt.

Rasam—A spicy soup made of lentils and tomatoes. Hot and sharp; served sometimes as an appetizer. A specialty of the South.

Rava—Farina.

Saffron—The stigma of the crocus plant.

Sambar—A lentil and vegetable preparation. It is sharp and spicy and is usually eaten with rice in South India.

Samosa—A thin pastry filled with boiled vegetable or minced meat and deep fried.

Sev—Salted, long, thin bits made of lentil flour.

Shami kebab—Made-up cutlets with minced meat and lentils.

Shrikhand—A sweet yogurt with liquid removed and flavored.

Snake gourd—Vegetable of a long snakelike shape.

Tamarind—A sour fruit used for curries, chutneys, etc.

Tandoori—Barbecued, spiced meat or fish.

Toddy—An alcoholic drink obtained from a variety of palm.

Turmeric—A yellow spice used for imparting a characteristic flavor and color. The root of a plant belonging to the ginger family.

Uppuma—A savory Southern dish made out of farina and lentils.

Vindaloo—A sour curry made of lamb, fish, shrimp, or pork, popular in the South.

Wada or *Pakora*—A made-up rissole of lentils or vegetables served as a snack.

Wark—Thin foil of silver or gold which is edible.

Yellow rice—Rice, flavored and colored with saffron or turmeric.

Zarda—A sweet *pulao* served at the end of a meal.

INDIAN RESTAURANTS IN THE UNITED STATES

Courtesy Government of India Tourist Office
19 East 49 Street, New York, N.Y.

IN NEW YORK CITY

Bit of Bali
127 West 43 Street, New York, N.Y. (LT 1-2288)

Ceylon India Inn
148 West 49 Street, New York, N.Y. (CO 5-9822)

Kashmir Restaurant
108 West 45 Street, New York, N.Y. (CI 7-8785)

Karachi Restaurant
144 West 46 Street, New York, N.Y. (CI 5-9643)

India Maharaja Restaurant
2487 Broadway, New York, N.Y. (EN 2-4554)

Taj Mahal Restaurant
201 East 34 Street, New York, N.Y. (MU 4-9895)

Punjab Restaurant
170 Bleeker Street, New York, N.Y. (AL 4-8855)

New Pakistan India Inn
West 110 Street & Eighth Avenue, New York, N.Y. (UN 4-9226)

Bombay India Restaurant
465 West 125 Street, New York, N.Y. (UN 4-9634)

East of Suez Inn
308 East 58 Street, New York, N.Y. (PL 9-4340)

Taj Mahal Restaurant
   13 Walnut Street, S., Philadelphia, Pa. (KI 5-0780)

India House Restaurant
   629 Washington Street, San Francisco, Calif. (EX 2-0744)

India Taj Restaurant
   825 Pacific Avenue, San Francisco, Calif. (EX 2-0089)

India Center
   4860 Sunset Boulevard & Vermont, Los Angeles, Calif.
   (NO 1-8006)

India Room
   2424 Wilshire Boulevard, Los Angeles, Calif. (483-7994)

OTHER TOURIST OFFICES IN NORTH AMERICA

685 Market Street, San Francisco 5, Calif. (EX 7-0066)

CANADA

177–179 King Street at University, Toronto 1, Canada
(EM 2-3188)

Index

Spiced, 68
Spiced Pot Roast, 68
Steak, 113
Beet Soup, 138
Bengal Chutney, 141
Besani Roti (Spiced Pancake Bread), 129
Bhaja-Maslar Tarkari (Eggplant), 88
Bhap-Chop (Spiced Lamb Chops), 106
Bhel Poori (Puffed Rice Salad), 192
Bhindi Kari (Okra Curry), 85
Bhune Kaju (Cashews), 194
Bhuni Kaleji (Chicken or Beef Liver), 47
Bhurta (Eggplant, Onion, and Tomato), 88
Biryani (Chicken and Rice), 162
Bombay Halwa, 200
Bonda (Spiced Potato Balls), 196
Boti Kebabs (Barbecued Beef or Lamb Squares on Skewers), 109
Bread: in Cream Sauce, Golden Fried, 206
Griddle, 129
Pancake, 126, 128
Puffs, Fried, 125
Spiced Pancake, 129
Stuffed Pancake, 127
Three Layer Griddle, 130
Brinjal Raita (Eggplant and Yogurt), 151
Broiled: Indian Shrimp, 73
Kebabs, 108
Buckra Aloo (Lamb and Potatoes), 64
Butlers Korma (Meat Curry), 71
Butty (Rice Salad), 170

Cabbage: Foogath, 86
and Rice, 166
Cakes: Banana, 173
Coconut, 188
Coconut and Fruit, 177
Deep Fried Sweet, 176
Farina, 183
Fried, 175
Fruit and Nut, 218
Hot, 191
Moon, 209
Potato, 191
Spice, 180
Steamed, 188
Steamed Coconut, 176
Sweet, 209
Sweet Butter, 173
Sweet Fried, 174, 215
Tapioca and Nut, 183
Calcutta Curry Mix, 34
Cardamom and Almond Halwa, 201
Carrot: Halwa, 199
and Onion Salad, 144
Cashews, 194
and Coconut Sweet, 203
Nut Snacks, 180
Sweet, 208
Cauliflower: Curry, 95
Eggs and, 102
and Peas, 96
Chandra Puli (Moon Cakes), 209
Cheenee Kuddoo (Sugar Squash), 210
Cheese: Fritters, 182
Pancakes, 179
and Rice, 157
and Vegetable Curry, 101
Chhanar: Dalna (Cheese and Vegetable Curry), 101

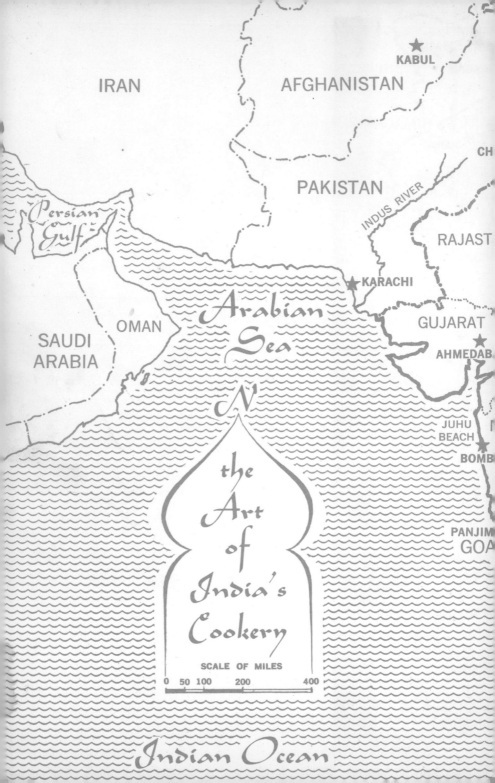